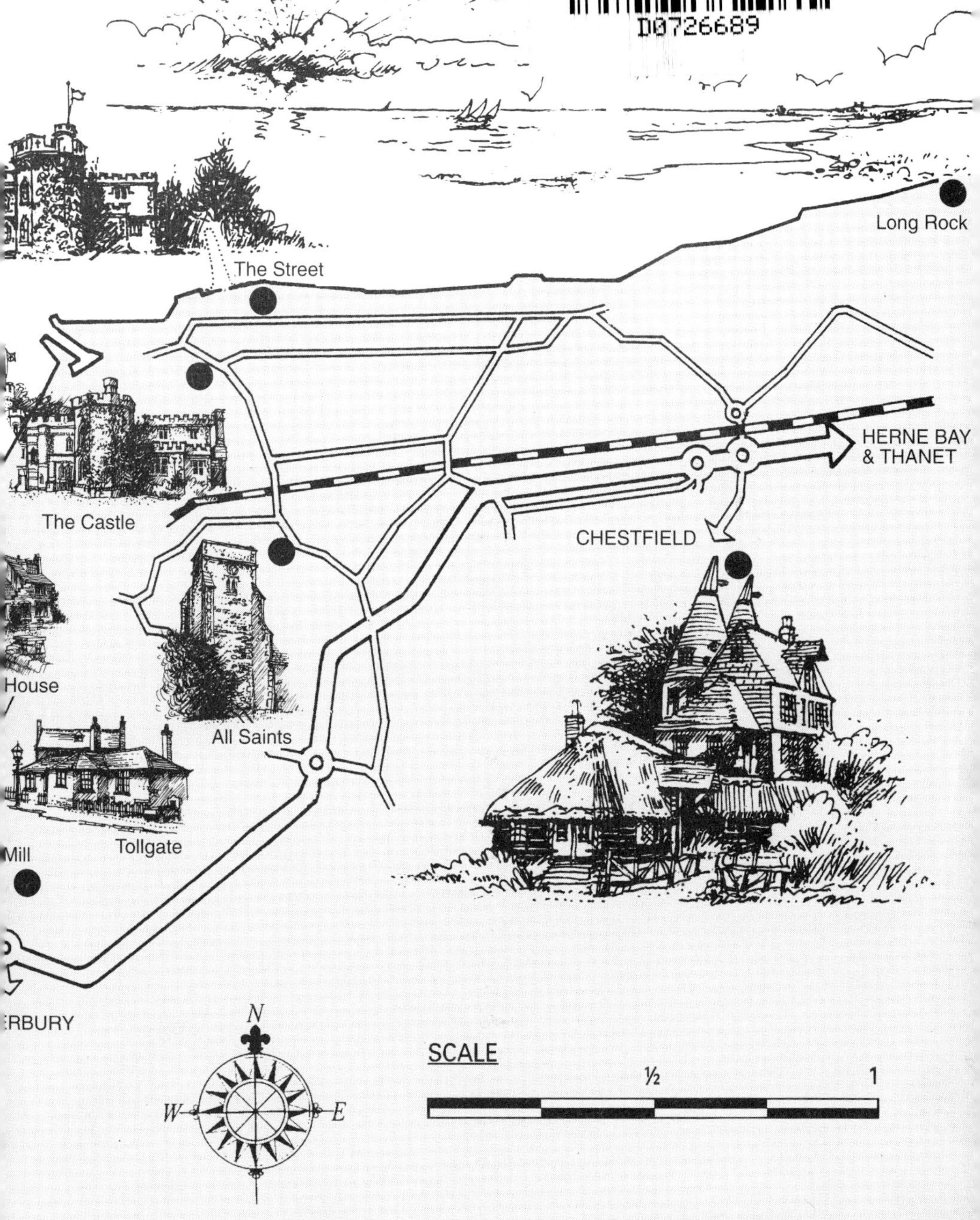
The Street
Long Rock
HERNE BAY
& THANET
The Castle
CHESTFIELD
House
All Saints
Tollgate
Mill
ERBURY
N
W
E
SCALE
½
1

History in WHITSTABLE

PLACES & PEOPLE

Geoffrey Pike
John Cann

Published by **Whitstable Improvement Trust**
34 Harbour Street, Whitstable, Kent CT5 1AJ
Registered Charity No. 1003120

This Edition February 2004

First Published November 1995

ISBN No. **0-9515828-5-2**

British Library Cataloguing in Publication Data.
A catalogue reference for this book is available from the British Library

Project Co-ordination and design	John Cann
Editor	Mike Page
Typesetting	Debbie Gregory
Printer	Oyster Press

DEDICATION

This book is dedicated to the following in appreciation of their contributions to the study of Whitstable's history:

Robert Goodsall F.R.I.B.A. 1891-1975
Douglas West A.B.I.P.P. 1904-1993
Wallace Harvey M.A.

Acknowledgements

Grateful acknowledgement is made to the following publishers for their permission to reproduce extended passages as indicated in the references:

Chatto & Windus: Laurence Irving, 'The Precarious Crust' 1971.

Pryor Publications: George and Greta Woodman, 'We Remember Whitstable' 2nd.Ed. 1988.

The following are thanked for making available source material:

Canterbury City Council
(deeds of the Harbour and The Castle).
Canterbury Library – The Local
Studies Collection.
Whitstable Library.

The Ancient Order of Foresters
(Mr. C. Sampson).
Mr. R. Carden and Mr & Mrs J. Hart
(for Edward Carden).
The Favourite Trust.
Mrs Manda Gifford (Whitstable Museum
Development Officer).
Harold Gough (Pudding Pan Rock).
Wallace Harvey (Whitstable archive).
Brian Porter (Graveney Boat and
Seasalter logboat).
Kenneth Reedie (Curator of Museums
and Galleries).
Mrs Beatrix Walsh (for the diaries of
Elizabeth Pearson).
Mrs Kath. Williamson
(for the tape of Mrs Kate Anderson).

References *to sources are placed at the end of each chapter - words printed in bold as an aid to ready identification of sources and notes. The following are noted by abbreviations:* AC Archaeologia Cantiana, WT The Whitstable Times

The Whitstable Improvement Trust is an independent Charitable Trust and Limited Company devoted to the careful preservation and the regeneration of Whitstable. It seeks to retain and care for the unique nature of the locality and its buildings, whilst creating an awareness of the town's historical past and the characters who have contributed to it. Initially funded by the city and county councils, the Trust now exists through its own resources and initiatives with the support of those who live and work in the town and its environs.

HISTORY IN WHITSTABLE: PLACES AND PEOPLE

Foreword

This book seeks to capture an enthusiasm and express an affection. Enthusiasm for searching out and assembling the history of that part of north Kent which stretches along the coast from Seasalter to Swalecliffe. And affection for the town of Whitstable which has expanded to embrace this area: its individuality and character, and its roots in the past. These are the qualities which author and artist have sought to convey through text and illustration.

Mention the name 'Whitstable' and the reply comes - 'Oysters!' Walk from the active harbour along the narrow lanes which parallel the shore - Sea Wall to the Horsebridge and beyond along Island Wall - and one is certainly aware of a maritime heritage in the fishermens' lofts and stores. The cottages and terraces, and the variety of small shops in Harbour Street, all speak, too, of a small Victorian town. And there are certainly oysters still available for sale.

But look around a little more widely and other features from the past now meet the eye. There on the hill is a windmill; in other places timbered buildings - are they old? There is the parish church - the tower at least looks ancient, but why is it well away from the centre of the town? Such questions suggest a more distant past surviving into present times; there is more to this area than a Victorian harbour, sea-faring and the dredging of oysters, though the last century certainly produced stirring times as we have recounted in our book 'Ales and Tales'.

'People and Places' is devised as a series of explorations: eleven historical features are used as starting points for delving into the past. Prehistoric artefacts, Roman pottery and a tenth-century boat are now all preserved in museums, but all the others chosen are part of the landscape today. For some the process of discovery itself is described: that chance observation, for example, which identified a medieval roof timber in a barn, and so saved from demolition the remains of an ancient manor house. Each of the features selected raises questions for investigation: its origin, its uses, and its role, and so the process of discovery moves outward to a wider association of people and community. Gradually a picture of a particular era in the local history emerges.

As in all explorations there are mysteries encountered - where, one would like to know, was located the medieval landing place called 'Graystone'? And there are surprises - it seems likely that the embryo Whitstable, the tiny fishing village of the eighteenth century was locally known as 'Harwich'.

Each chapter can be read independently but they have been arranged so that a chronological sequence emerges, as the following 'Contents' page illustrates. We begin in the Palaeolithic with the flint tools of prehistoric man and end with film actor Peter Cushing who died in 1994, having made his home in Whitstable for forty years. 'Places and People' is not a recital of dry facts and dates, but an attempt to recreate the story of people and their times within this local area. In the earlier history they are shadowy figures, but later they come alive as individual characters: the boy Laurence Irving at play in the windmill; the life of a girl 'in service' up at the Castle; the intriguing period of William Joyce's stay in the town (the Lord Haw-Haw of the wartime years); and 'Biscuits' Goldfinch, a Whitstable 'native', a great eccentric, whose life spanned almost a century from 1861 to 1956.

Throughout the book the pages are enlivened with line drawings illustrating details and providing imaginative reconstructions of background scenes or important events. It is hoped that, with its individual style of presenting local history, this book will appeal equally to local residents and the more general reader. For those with a more specific interest in local history each chapter is concluded with references and notes detailing the range of sources which have been used, and the index provides a guide on a more thematic basis.

Whitstable is a small town, in statistical terms typical of many, but a closer acquaintance reveals an individuality and a fascinating history which is gradually unfolded in the following chapters.

CONTENTS

1 THE PREHISTORIC SITE AT SWALECLIFFE

At the turn of the century in July 1900, Mr Collard's thoughts may quite naturally have been turned towards the years ahead. If so then what he found on his morning's walk from Herne Bay to Whitstable certainly projected him back into the distant past[1].

As he strolled along the beach at Swalecliffe he noticed something protruding near the base of the low cliff, and on closer examination it appeared to have a bone-like character. Later that day the object, slowly eased out from the surrounding clay, was revealed to be a huge, slightly curved, fossil trunk some nine feet in length, eighteen inches round at the thickest part, and weighing over 70 pounds. It was in a good state of preservation

Mammoth hunters at Swalecliffe

though broken in two places. Undoubtedly this came from that extinct creature of the Ice Age – the Mammoth.

Such a splendid specimen was a great find, but not altogether surprising, for these cliffs, like those beyond Herne Bay, were already noted for producing quantities of fossil remains.

At this time the coastline at Swalecliffe was untouched by sea-defence works, so the low cliffs were totally exposed, rapidly crumbling, and retreating under attack from the sea. Much as today towards the Priest and Sow corner, that curiously named spot in Tankerton, they rose about 25 feet high, then declined eastwards to about ten feet, with a continuing gentle slope down to the slightly incised channel of the Swale Brook. With this continuing erosion, the geological structure of the cliff face was made very clear and accessible. This enabled one enthusiastic local resident, Mr EH

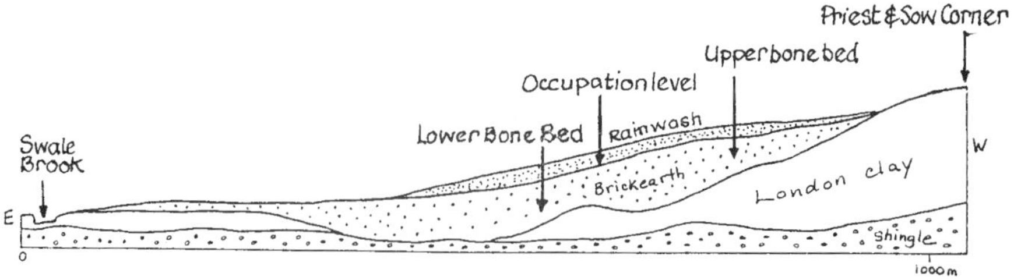

Swalecliffe: generalised cliff section.

Worsfold, to spend many years collecting and studying the animal bones and the tools of prehistoric man which he found there[2].

As shown in the diagram, at the western end of this area the bedrock London clay is at the surface. It then dips down eastwards to be covered with brickearth in a layer of increasing depth, at one point appearing to fill an old channel cut into the clay beneath. The brickearth is composed of fine clay with pockets of sand and gravels. It was laid down during the later stages of the Ice Age, that long period when four times the great sheets of ice and glaciers formed over the central and northern parts of the country. The brickearth was probably formed by slumping and flooding, spreading fine material which had thawed out of the ice and frozen ground. These deposits at Swalecliffe may be related to a river system which flowed across this area into the North Sea plain (sea level having fallen dramatically with the water held by the icecaps and glaciers)[3]. The brickearth, as its name indicates, was often used in the making of bricks – as indeed it was close by at Swalecliffe.

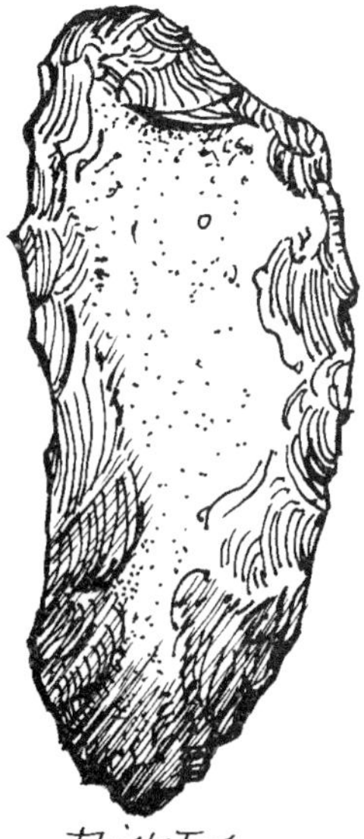
Flint Tool.

Above the brickearth was a capping layer forming the ground surface, varying in thickness from one to four feet. This was composed of a sticky clay which had been produced by later rainwash down the slope.

It was from the exposed face of these layers in the cliffs that fossil bones of a variety of animals, now mainly extinct, could be collected, together with evidence of prehistoric man.

From the higher level of the brickearth deposits came remains of the straight-tusked elephant, the giant ox and red deer which would have grazed on a mixture of grassland and woodland, suggesting relatively warm climatic conditions. This would have been the inter-glacial period which followed the retreat of the third great glaciation. Further east in the cliff face at a lower level and of a later age was another 'bone bed' containing the remains of mammoths, woolly rhinoceros, cave hyena and horse. These animals suggest sub-arctic conditions, similar to Finland today, with scrubland of coarse grass, tough bushes and scattered stands of pine and fir. These features indicate the onset at about 70,000BC of the last glacial epoch which may be said to have ended in 8000BC.

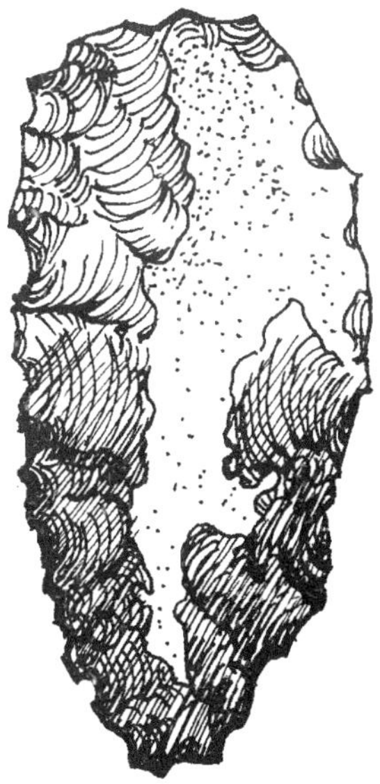

Flint tool

On the beach below the cliffs Mr Worsfold and other local residents were able to collect flint implements, evidence of the presence of prehistoric man. These had clearly been washed out of the cliffs during their erosion. Such tools are almost the sole evidence of early man and the gradual changes and sophistication of the techniques employed in their manufacture are used to chronicle the human history of this remote period[4].

An implement was made by selecting a block of natural flint and fashioning it into the required shape by striking it, usually with a stone as a hammer, so that the flakes were detached. This fracturing was a characteristic of flint. With skill, a suitable shape for the hand and the required sharp cutting edge could be produced quite rapidly. The earliest known tools are very sim-

Flint Working

ple, employing a crude technique, but as skill advanced over thousands of years an increasing range of forms was produced, their superb shaping showing an aesthetic sense as well as immense practicality. Even the early tools can be distinguished from natural chipping by the uniformity of the flaking - all from one direction - and when grasped, by their fit to the hand.

The earliest tool found by Mr Worsfold in this area was a beautifully shaped hand-axe belonging to the type known as Acheulian (from the Lower Palaeolithic Period), just over two inches long. This probably dates to the third inter-glacial, contemporary therefore with the higher level bone-bed. At Swanscombe in Kent skull fragments have been discovered associated with considerable evidence of this prehistoric period. They probably belonged to a man in his early twenties and at a quarter of a million years old, give us evidence of one of the earliest known ancestors of modern man.

In the capping layer of hill-wash material (see diagram) the exposed cliff showed three saucer shaped bands composed of carbonized material containing pebbles used as pot-boilers, flint flakes and a wide range of flint implements: blades, scrapers, borers, and even primitive arrow heads. These were evidence of occupation sites of the later period known as Maglemosian. Around 8000BC the climate began improving as the ice receded. The landscape was becoming forested and lighter game such as red deer and the wild ox were important for food supply, and the rivers also gave a plentiful supply of fish and water fowl. The typical tools now were very different: composed of tiny sharp flints – known as microliths – which were mounted in wooden shafts to make composite tools such as saws and knives. The Maglemosian people had certainly domesticated the dog and their use of fire to make clearings in the forest suggests that they may have developed the herding of animals such as deer – the first step towards agriculture. These newcomers were the last to reach Britain by land, for, by 6000BC, the North Sea plain had been flooded in the changes in land/sea level which followed the final period of glaciation. In a simi-

Thames Valley Pick

lar way southern England was separated from the continent with the formation of the English Channel.

Among the many flint tools obtained from Tankerton bay, one, known as the Thames Valley Pick, is interesting as its particular technique is only found in the Thames area. These are implements up to eight inches long, whose use is uncertain. One was discovered by Mr Worsfold in a large freshly-fallen lump of the hill-wash material, so identifying it with the Maglemosian layer. This green coated flint had been sharpened at one end but the other remained unworked: it appeared to have been rejected after a misdirected blow marred its shape and usefulness. Since many detached flakes from similar implements were found in the occupation layers, it would seem that they were manufactured here.

It is not until the later Bronze Age, perhaps about the tenth century BC that evidence of occupation appears again at Swalecliffe. Now both farming and metal working were well established. Portions of a cinerary urn have been found containing bones and ashes and close by an arrowhead and an adze made of the stone diorite[5]. Then in February 1922 a cliff fall revealed a sensational hoard of bronze objects: socketed and winged axes, sword and spearheads together with founders' metal[6]. One can only speculate on the circumstances which led to the burial and abandonment of items which represented considerable wealth. Many of these items of fine quality are now in the British Museum collection. Further evidence of Bronze Age occupation in this area was shown by the discovery in 1975 of a pottery vessel on the foreshore called a 'beaker', which was typical of people who lived in coastal areas from East Anglia to Sussex from 1800BC[7].

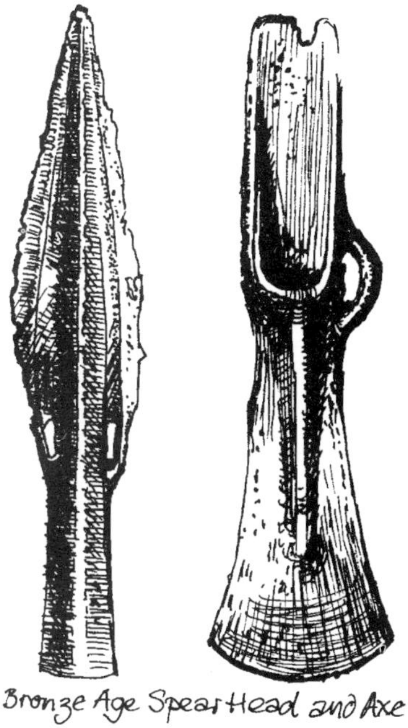

Bronze Age Spear Head and Axe

Extending seaward of these prehistoric sites at Swalecliffe are the shallow waters of the Kentish Flats, at low tide covered on average by no more than one and half fathoms of water. The 'shallows' stretch for some three miles off the coastline of today, the submerged region being about

20 miles across. Relative changes in land/sea level have resulted in a gradual rise in sea-level, resulting in the flooding of what was originally dry land. This process, so significant in the evolution of the local topography and therefore its human history, is discussed more fully in the following chapters.

Increasingly it is being realised that this off-shore zone contains a wealth of archaeological material: some deposited from the erosion of the low cliffs (now largely ended by coastal protection works), and some revealed in situ as the advancing sea has planed down the old land surfaces. To this can also be added knowledge of more recent times from the exploration of the wrecks whose remains lie embedded in the sand and mud.

Here at Swalecliffe examination of the foreshore at Long Rock indicates that originally the Swale Brook had a more northerly course and along the

abandoned bed a variety of archaeological material is evident: some probably rubbish deposited by the stream, but some suggests prehistoric occupation along its banks[8].

Mammoth tusks may be very exciting to find, but it is really the careful collection and systematic recording of finds which will gradually piece together the history of this local area and that great extension of the land which now lies covered by the sea.

References

1. WT 14.7.1900. also reported in 1930, a find at a depth of 25ft in the cliff face - 2 molars, 3 tusks, and a tusk 9ft long, although only a part of this could be extracted: WT 1.3.1930.
2. **Worsfold** EH, 'An examination of the contents of the brick-earths and gravels of Tankerton Bay, Swalecliffe, Kent': Proc. Geol. Assn. v.37, pp. 326-339.
3. Holmes SC, '**Geology of the country around Faversham**', Geological Survey of Great Britain, Memoir for sheet 273, HMSO 1981, pp. 89-91.
4. Laing L & J., 'The **Origins of Britain**', Routledge and Kegan Paul 1979.
   Drewett P, Rudling D, Gardiner M, '**The South East to AD1000**'. Longmans 1988
5. Worsfold EH, ref. 2 above.
6. **Bronze Age Hoard** - details are recorded on the Ordnance Survey Archaeology Index Sheet, Canterbury Library Local Studies collection, and Whitstable Library map collection.
7. Reedie K, AC v. XCII 1976, p. 253, and v. XCIII 1977 p. 212. Bronze Age Beaker.
8. Macpherson-Grant N, 'Long Rock, Swalecliffe', report Canterbury Archaeological Trust 1992, Fieldwork report: 28.

2 PUDDING PAN ROCK AND A ROMAN WRECK

It was a traditional custom in Whitstable, certainly to the end of the nineteenth century, to celebrate Ash Wednesday by baking a specially rich pie: 'Make a pastry case and fill it with a mixture of rice, blended with milk, eggs, butter and sugar; flavour it with a little bay and pinch of spice; sprinkle with currants and grated nutmeg; then bake until a golden brown.'[1]

There was nothing particularly unusual about such a folk custom except for one item: in Whitstable the pie was preferably baked in a broad dish or platter of Roman Samian ware[2]. This curious feature of fishermen's cottages having Roman pots in use in their kitchens attracted the attention of one of those antiquarians who typified late eighteenth century society. It was Thomas Pownell who reported on these circumstances in the learned journal 'Archaeologia' in 1778. He described how six years earlier his brother had gone out with local fishermen to the location where such pottery was frequently brought up in their dredges and trawls. The most prolific source was around the shoal appropriately named Pudding Pan Rock[3].

On this investigation soundings were taken, indicating what appeared to be a rock-like protrusion covered only by nine feet of water at low tide, and

A Roman Merchant Ship founders at Pudding Pan Boulders

in size not much larger than the hull of a small ship. Dredging in this area produced three complete pans, many fragments and 'a half hundred fragments of brickwork "cemented" together'. Pownell's account excited interest in antiquarian circles and various theories were advanced to account for this spread of Roman pottery across the sea-bed.

In the 1790s, Hasted, the great Kent historian, commented[4]: 'The traditional story of the country (and tradition has in general found to have some truth for its foundation, however misrepresented by ignorance and a series of time) that some vessel, freighted with this manufacture, was many ages ago cast away on this rock, and its lading dispersed on and about it by the force of the waves, from time to time.'

As a result, he explained: '...the circumstances of their being found coming to the knowledge of the curious antiquarians, they have been in general sought out and purchased by them, and are now preserved among their respective collections.'

It is estimated that at least 300 complete specimens of the ware have been brought ashore, and it is probable that others were discreetly sold in addition[5]. Mr William Holden of Whitstable made a collection of some 130 pots which was later divided between the British Museum and the local historical exhibits which are now in the town's museum[6]. Most have come from the vicinity of Pudding Pan, though some have been recovered over a wider area, doubtless carried some distance when caught in the fishermen's dredges and trawls.

To consider the exact origin of the pottery and the nature of Pudding Pan one must consider the topography of this area in Roman times. Particularly in the marshes along the lower Medway, archaeologists have found widespread evidence of occupation of this period now some ten feet below high tide level[7]. Presuming that the land surface was above any flooding at the highest Spring tide level, this would mean it stood some four or five feet at least above the normal tides. So the net result is to demonstrate a subsidence of the land surface since Roman times of the order of fifteen feet. Other archaeological work around the Thames estuary has confirmed this general conclusion. The explanation lies in the geological process of the gradual sinking of the whole of the North Sea basin; in a sense the British Isles are tilting – slowly rising on the west and subsiding on the east. It is this factor which explains the long estuaries from the Thames northwards: they have been formed by the drowning of the lower portions of the river valleys.

Roman Pottery C. AD. 170
Dredged from the Pan Shoal.

In the local area, if sea level is lowered by fifteen feet, then the wide stretch of shallow water, the Kentish Flats, becomes dry land. At low tide the Flats are only covered on average by one and a half fathoms of water and on the northern edge there is a very clearly defined drop into deeper water which must represent the line of the original river channel. The phenomenally low tide of March 1896 revealed the sea-bed surface for well over a mile, and as people walked out they found the trunks of large trees which lay where they had fallen, and it is not uncommon today for pieces of semi-fossilised wood to be cast up on the local beaches; clearly demonstrating that this was once a dry land surface[8].

It can be estimated that, on average, the Roman coastline was some two

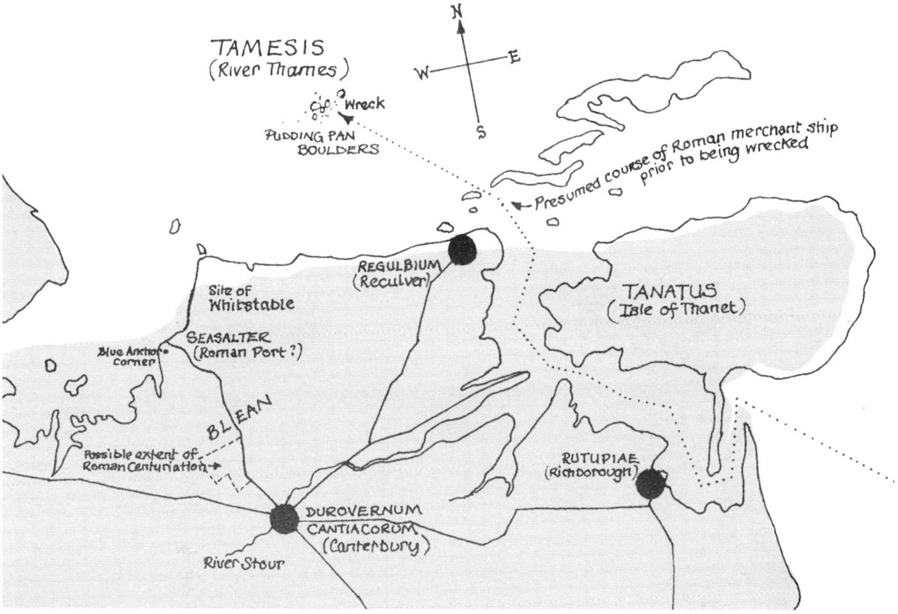

Coastline N.E. Kent in Roman Times (shaded area shows modern Kent Coastline).

and a half to three miles further out than its present position, so Pudding Pan at about four miles must have been either a peninsula projecting northwards, or more probably an island on the edge of the fairly narrow navigable channel which then existed[9].

At least 30 different potters' names have been identified on the Pudding Pan ware and these have been traced to the major pottery centre around Lezoux in the Allier valley near Clermont Ferrand in central France. This trade in plain utilitarian pottery dominated the market in Britain towards the end of the second century AD. A likely date for this cargo is thought to be around AD170[10].

Most probably this was a vessel trading into the Thames for the London market which foundered on the Pan shoal, and as the vessel disintegrated its cargo has gradually scattered. The report by Pownell of bricks and the occasional find of tiles have led to speculation that there was some kind of beacon or lighthouse built here to guide and warn ships. However, large concretions do, in fact, occur naturally in the bedrock clay and when exposed give rise to large stony areas. Such material may have been mistaken for building debris. This 'boulder stone' was at one time collected at Whitstable and elsewhere for the making of a cement called 'compo' which was used like stucco to cover the brickwork on buildings[11].

With archaeological interest aroused, reports of other incidental finds have been made, though unfortunately often with only the vaguest or totally unrecorded location. Thus there were further descriptions of 'large masses of brick, stone masonry and roofing tiles' made in 1885[12]. These, together with the number of complete pots and fragments found, led to the proposal that they represented 'the wreck of a town or village of potters' rather than a shipwreck. In his collection at Whitstable Mr Holden had a number of other types of Roman pottery, much finer than the Pan Samian ware which had been brought up from the Flats: described as 'figured ware' and 'Tuscan ware' and 'two fine examples of Roman household shallow dishes with spouts, in the form of Mortaria, in black ware'. And as further evidence of Roman occupation he cited a Roman cistern which had come from a little east of the shingle bank, the Street, about a mile from the shore, and also many roof tiles which he had collected from the Whitstable fishermen.

Without the opportunity to examine such evidence in situ care must be taken not to conclude that they represent proof of occupation out on the old land surface. Items such as the roof tiles might well have been dumped overboard in material used as ship's ballast; tiles were also used on board Roman vessels to form cooking hearths, so those in the vicinity of Pan Rock could have come from a wreck. There is, of course, the long tradition of an oyster fishery along this coast in Roman times, though hardly to produce 'Whitstable' oysters as written in many guidebooks[13]. Certainly the Romans had an immense fondness for oysters and regarded those from 'Rutupiae' (the modern Richborough) as being amongst the best; so much so that they were transported back to the city of Rome itself. With a major Roman city nearby at Canterbury, where oyster shells are found in abundance on excavation sites, suitable local waters would undoubtedly have been exploited. Evidence of such fishermen was found by Thomas Porter in 1970 when, at an extremely low tide, he found the well-preserved remains of a dug-out or logboat exposed in the mud about a mile off the Seasalter coast[14]. This was made of oak, nearly nineteen feet long and three feet wide, with spoon-shaped ends. Unfortunately preservation action was not taken and it later disappeared; carbon dating of a sample of the wood gave a date of around AD200.

There has always been a strong local tradition that the road from Blean down to the Seasalter shore via Foxe's Cross was of Roman origin. At Blue Anchor corner the road heads straight out towards the sea and then is forced to bend sharply inside the fourteenth century sea wall. Support for a Roman connection has recently come from the work of the Blean Research Group who have identified in the woods lines of low earthworks forming a grid pattern strongly suggestive of the Roman field system called 'centuriation'[15]. These blocks of land were marked out in this way in many parts of the Empire as small-holding grants for retired soldiers – 'centurians'. Now this grid pattern aligns directly to the road running through Blean, indicating it was contemporary. This road would therefore have run from the city gate in the position of the medieval West Gate through Blean and then down into Seasalter and out, perhaps, to a creek cutting into the flat coastal plain. And here again we may follow Hasted's advice not to disdain local traditions, for fishermen used to tell 'that far out in the tideway there are large stones, indicating that once, before the erosion of the coast set in there was a landing place for shipping'[16]. It is conceivable that there was a minor Roman port off the present coast at Seasalter.

If we come ashore, so to speak, then little evidence has been found of the Roman period to the north of what are now the Blean woods (at that time probably heathland with stands of oak trees). In 1989 on the southern side of the Seasalter levels, at Lavender Farm, the removal of topsoil revealed a site from which industrial refuse found suggested iron working in the vicinity, using local timber for charcoal and ironstone perhaps imported through one of the creeks which then crossed the marshy country, stretching out to the more distant coastline[17]. Then evidence of a more substantial building was excavated in 1961 at South Street on the fringe of the woods[18]. There was uncovered a small sunken chamber with walling made up of tiles and in the infilling were fragments of painted plaster suggesting domestic accommodation above. Pottery waste in and around the site showed the presence here of a tile kiln: another local industrial unit. Finally at Highgate Farm at Chestfield, a variety of post holes, pit and ditches, together with artefacts from the Neolithic period onward indicated an agricultural site occupied over a long period, and with evidence of a field system of Roman age[19]. This relatively simple farming probably typified that prevailing across the fairly open country lying north of the Blean: a topic more fully discussed in the course of Chapter Five.

With the development of aqualung diving equipment numerous amateur expeditions have been organised to try to solve the mystery of the Pudding Pan Rock and Sands by locating the supposed Roman wreck. Activity seems to have been stimulated after a piece of the pottery was used in 1955 to puzzle the experts in a popular quiz programme 'Animal, Vegetable, Mineral'. Alas, strong currents and murky waters have defeated all attempts. As one group reported: 'The sea was so bad many of us were sick. Visibility at 30ft down was nil, so we had to try dredging in the end. The tile was the only result!'[20] Since 1988 a more professional interest has been taken by marine archaeologists using sonar equipment, but without result so far[21]. To date it remains, as one newspaper report was headlined: 'Search for Lost Ship. But Sea Retains Its Secrets'[22].

References

1. Whitstable Museum. Labelling with the display of **Pudding Pan pottery**.
2. Collard AO, '**The Oyster and Dredgers of Whitstable**', Collard London 1902, p.81.
3. Pownell T, 'Memoire on the Roman Earthen Ware fished up within the mouth of the River Thames', Archaeologia v.V 1778, p.282.
4. **Hasted** E, 'The History and Topographical survey of the County of Kent' 2nd ed in 12 vols. 1797 -1801, edition EP Publishing Ltd 1972, p.508.
5. Smith CR, 'Mr Teanby's collection of Romano-British Pottery, AC v. XI 1877, pp.118-120.
   Payne G, 'Potters Names and Marks on Pseudo-Samian Ware found in Kent', AC v. XVII 1887, p.153.
   '**Victoria County History of Kent**', St Catharine's Press, London 1932, v.3 p.165.
   Smith R, summary in Proc. Soc. Antiq., London, 2nd series 1906, v.XXI p.268 and XXII p.395.
6. Goodsall R, '**Whitstable, Seasalter and Swalecliffe – The History** of Three Kent Parishes', Canterbury 1938 pp.7-9 (The Holden collection, listing potters' names.).
7. Evans JH, '**Archaeological Horizons in the North Kent marshes**', AC v. LXVI, 1953, p.103.
8. Ackeroyd A, '**Archaeological and Historical evidence for subsidence in southern Britain**', Phil. Trans. Royal Soc. London v. CCLXXII 1972 p.151-69.
   So CL, 'Early **Coast Recession around Reculver**, Kent, AC v. LXXXVI 1971 p.95.
   Collard AO, ref 2. above.
9. So CL ref. 8. above.
   Holmes SC, '**Geology of the Country around Faversham**', Geological Survey of Great Britain: Memoir for sheet 273, HMSO 1981, p.103.
10. Frere S, 'Britannia: '**A History of Roman Britain**' Routledge and Kegan Paul, London 1978 p.327.
11. Wrightson J, 'The Railway Companion', Canterbury 1836 p.21 (Canterbury Local Studies Collection).
12. Astbury AK, 'Estuary: **Land and water in the lower Thames basin**', Carnforth Press 1980, quoting report by FJ Spurrell.
13. Pike G, Cann J, Lambert R, '**Oysters and Dredgermen**', Compass Publications 1992, Whitstable, p.12 and refs. (See also Ch 9, The 'Favourite' Oyster Smack).
14. WT 20.10.1988.

McGrail S, '**Logboats** of England and Wales, part 1, BAR British Series 51 (1), 1978, p.267.

15. Wheaton A, 'Report of the **Blean Woods** Archaeological Research Group' Spring 1989, p.9. (Canterbury Library Local Studies collection).
16. Lugard C, '**Seasalter, Manor and Parish**', Whitstable n/d. In the 'Foreword' by Rev. E Thompson.
    The continuation of fish trading at Seasalter is illustrated by a **coins find**. Thirty seven were found ranging in date from 1072 to 1422; of these 29 could have been contemporary, dating from 1180 to 1247, and would suggest the loss of a purse, perhaps. WT 9.7.1987, report of the Inquest on the find.
17. Rady J, '**Lavender Farm**', report Canterbury Archaeological Trust 1989, section 24.
18. WT 24.6.61.
19. Bennett P and Blockley P, 'District Report', Report Canterbury Archaeological Trust 1986-87 p.22. (**Highgate Farm**.)
    WT 13.11.86.
20. WT 5.3.55 (TV programme).
    Kent Express, 16.9.55 (Underwater Explorers).
21. **Archaeological Diving Unit**, University of St Andrews: 'We have a fat file on 'Pudding Pan' largely made up of information produced by various investigators, including two dissertations by university students, as well as the published information. Almost every year we hear of new searches but as far as we are aware nothing from the Roman period has ever been found during these deliberate searches. Whereas fishermen occasionally recover material in their nets by chance.' (Information: Martin Dean)
22. Herne Bay Press 12.5.61.

3 THE GRAVENEY BOAT

In September 1970 a great discovery was made in the bleak open country of Graveney Marsh. Slowly and painstakingly a team of archaeologists exposed beneath some two metres of the surface clay a pattern of timbers forming the outline of an ancient boat. This was an exciting find which would add much to the existing limited knowledge of early craft in our waters, and also provide clues to local history in the area around Seasalter[1].

The discovery of an ancient
boat at Graveney Marshes.

As so often chance was the major factor in making this find. Mr Roy Boulting was at work with his mechanical excavator deepening and widening the Hammond Drain, one of the network of channels draining this marshy countryside. A sudden bump indicated an obstruction and on examination it proved to be a large balk of timber, set well down, suggesting something long buried. With commendable foresight he ceased work and reported his discovery to the supervisor. Local archaeologists were quickly summoned to the scene and recognised that here was something demanding further investigation.

Careful stripping by the mechanical excavator of the overlying clay gradually revealed the tips of two lines of timbers, surely the side planks of a boat, and the heavy timber showing at one end must then be the sternpost. The importance of the find was now clear and a team of highly experienced archaeologists assembled to undertake the excavation. As the timbers were exposed and the infill removed various objects were found within the boat: animal bones, fragments of lava and Roman tiles, pieces of Kentish ragstone, some pebbles and a few sherds of pottery; items which might yield clues to the use of this craft and the people who manned her.

Removing the clay from around the boat produced another fascinating

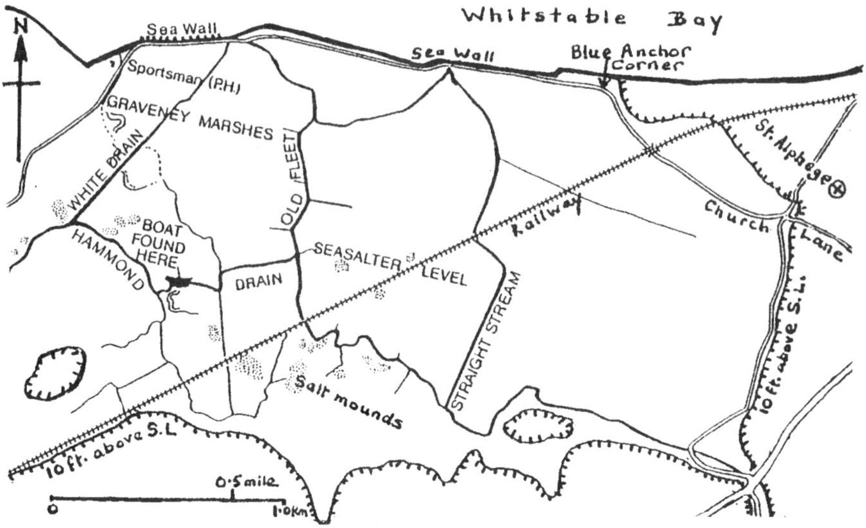

Site of Graveney Boat.

discovery. It had been supported by substantial pointed stakes driven into the ground on each side, and it rested on a layer of sticks. This then was not an accidental abandonment or a wreck but a careful laying-up of the vessel. With the survival of so much of the timber structure the decision was taken that the Graveney boat warranted detailed study requiring its removal and preservation. Here was something not only of great interest to professionals but a generally fascinating artefact from the past.

Lifting the timbers intact and reassembling them was a task requiring absolute precision, made particularly difficult by the remoteness of the site and the boggy clay ground. Speed was essential, though water was pumped on to the wood to prevent it drying out. From some 700 measurements a detailed plan was produced, a photographic record was made of every minute feature, and plaster of Paris was used to record a mould of the structure. Then the timbers were dismantled piece by piece, again with every stage carefully recorded. For the study of the wider context samples of soil were taken from the bottom infill, from between the timbers and from the clay around and beneath the boat. After thirteen days of strenuous activity the large keel piece was lifted and the operation on site completed.

With the boat safely in storage a variety of specialists began work on analysing and evaluating all the evidence which the boat and its excavation presented. In due course a detailed technical report was published. A replica of the boat is on view in the National Maritime Museum.

Immediately the intriguing question was asked: 'How old is the Graveney boat?' Initial suggestions ranged from the Roman period to the early medieval, for the basic structure of this kind of craft changed little over many centuries. Scientific analysis provided the answer: the Carbon 14 technique suggested the latter half of the ninth century and this was confirmed by tree-ring study of the planking which gave a date of AD927. So on balance it seemed that the boat was constructed around AD900 and similar analysis of the brushwood sticks indicated that it was dragged up to this situation about 40 years later. The Graveney boat dated from the late Saxon period.

What then can we learn about the construction and appearance of the Graveney boat? At some stage it had lost the bow and about one third of its length; internal fittings had been removed, and later the timbers had been cut off down to the water line. Originally the boat was just over fourteen metres in length with a beam of 3.9 metres. It was clinker-built with a stout backbone of keel and stems fore and aft, to which the planks were attached in overlapping sequence, fixed together with iron nails and made watertight by plugging with strands of sheeps' wool and a tar of some vegetable origin. This shell was then held inside with a series of cross frames, each secured in position by wooden trenails or bungs driven through the planking from the outside and each secured on the inner side of the frame by splitting wth a long oak wedge. These were then cut flush inside but projected as knobs along the outside of the boat.

This was clearly a stoutly built craft, designed to carry a heavy cargo with a minimum of draught, so that it could operate in shallow creeks and also negotiate rougher seas across to the continent. In design both bow and stern would have shown raking or sweeping upwards as shown on the illustration of the Faversham seal. It is unlikely that as a simple trading vessel these would have ended in decorative heads. Most probably there was a single mast supported

Faversham Seal

The Graveney Boat and site – artist's interpretation

with a good number of stays, and a square sail possibly made of wool. The ship most likely relied on a steering oar in calm conditions but used a side rudder in rougher waters.

Next one may look at the evidence for the apparent abandonment of this vessel. The general condition of the planking appeared sound, showing comparatively little sign of heavy wear and tear, suggesting that it was usually beached on soft muddy shores. Closer examination, however, revealed a serious crack in the keel which had been patched up by caulking and probably a metal plate. The absence of internal fixtures suggested that the boat had been adapted rather as a barge for the calm conditions of local estuaries. The presence of the underlying bed of branches supporting the hull on the soft mud, the thick stakes holding it in place, and the nearby mooring posts and signs of a timber stand - all these factors indicated that this site was a local landing place on to which the boat had been hauled. Indeed, traces of a rope which could have been so used remained attached to the keel.

Clearly, this would have been a suitable place at which to carry out further repairs. It is an interesting thought that it might even have been constructed here originally: the necessary oak from the Blean and willow from the marsh would have been readily available. Illustrations of this period show that boats of similar design were typical of this coast. Why then was the boat eventually abandoned? The answer to this may relate to the unsettled times with raids by the Vikings. The hacking away of the upper sides is difficult to date, and the missing section was probably destroyed fairly recently when the drain was widened.

From the artefacts found in the Graveney boat and the analysis of soil samples for plant remains some evidence was found for its usage. The fragments and chips of lava clearly indicated the carriage of circular querns for grinding corn, a very common import at this time from the middle Rhine area. The stout hull of the boat would have been well suited to such a bulky cargo. The other significant evidence came from the fossilised hops both from inside the boat and scattered widely across the brushwood platform, showing that this must have been the final cargo. We know that the brewery at Christ Church Priory at Canterbury was famous at this time, and they were the owners of this land at Graveney marsh. And as illustrated in Chapter Two there was a routeway from the city down to the shore at Seasalter even in Roman times. One may assume therefore that Canterbury was the destination of this cargo of hops.

This is an exciting conclusion, for this would be the first firm evidence for the use of hops in brewing in England.

Of the other items in the boat, the pottery was part of a cooking pot originating in France or Belgium. These were mainly imported through 'Hamwih" (Saxon Southampton). The bones were of sheep, goat, pig and cattle; and the remainder were probably remnants of ballast.

Put together, then, the material gathered in the excavation suggests that the Graveney boat was originally built for cross-Channel trade, and then, after sustaining severe damage, was patched up to work along the local coast and estuaries.

Considering next the situation of the boat, the evidence showed that it had been pulled up on a simple landing stage just above the level of an adjacent watercourse. Yet it was found beneath some two metres of estuarine clay and about a kilometre inland from today's high water mark. Clearly considerable changes have taken place in the coastline here since the tenth century. As discussed in Chapters One and Two, along the Thames estuary

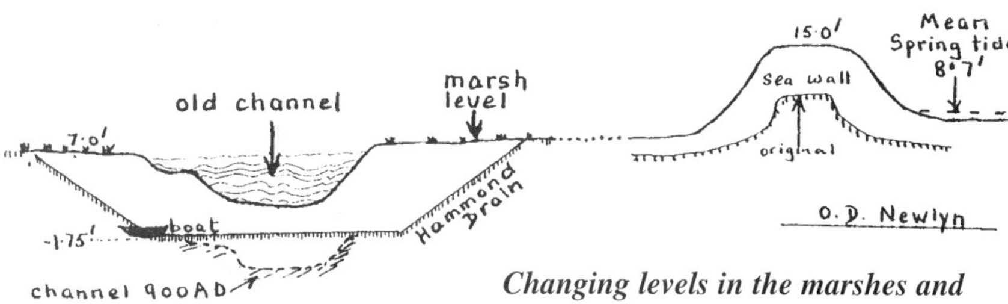

Changing levels in the marshes and positioning of Graveney Boat.

complex factors have affected relative land and sea levels[2].

Around AD900, with a relatively lower sea level and higher land level, this area of the Seasalter Levels and Graveney marshes would have been low-lying marshland merging into saltmarsh along the winding streams and creeks and stretching out across the present coastal flats to a coastline much further out. At periods of high tide the interaction between the salt water and the silt-laden streams would have caused continuing deposition, slowly raising the level of the marsh and silting up the creeks and channels. Shallow draught boats could penetrate some distance inland at this time, although the Saxon name for Graveney - 'Grafanea' - meaning a 'stream that feeds a canal', or a 'dug river' - shows that navigation problems were already becoming apparent.

These wide stretches of coastal marsh were a valued economic resource in Saxon times; indeed, they remain so today. Then in summer at least they provided extensive areas of first-class grazing especially for sheep[3]. Salt-making was very important as shown by references in Anglo-Saxon charters detailing 'sealterns' (salt houses) and emphasising the rights to take wood from the Blean to evaporate the brine[4]. Local salt production is listed in the Domesday Book and, of course, the very name 'Seasalter' derives from the Saxon 'sealterna steallas', meaning the salthouse by the sea. Fishing must also have been important both in the streams and along the coastline: eight fisheries are recorded under Seasalter in Domesday Book.

The full Domesday entry for Seasalter is somewhat puzzling[5]. The general entries are straightforward recording that the manor has one plough (indicating the size of a holding) and 48 smallholders are also reckoned as one plough; there is woodland for ten pigs and there is a church. The value of the manor is estimated to have risen from 25 shillings before the Conquest to 100 shillings in 1086. However this manorial description does not warrant the next entry, describing Seasalter as 'a small Borough... which belongs to the Archbishop's own kitchen'; for elsewhere the term 'borough' refers to important towns. The designation may perhaps have its roots in earlier Saxon times when certain places had special privileges as organised trading points or 'wics'. Some of these grew into towns but others - and perhaps this is one - did not[6]. Yet some of the old significance remained attached to Seasalter even though by the eleventh century coastal changes had brought its trading function to an end. Indeed this special nature of Seasalter continued for centuries, for, unlike surrounding parishes, this area

St. Alphege Church
from a map of 1770

remained a separate entity, a Liberty, and did not become part of the larger administrative unit, the 'Hundred' (see Chapter Four). Seasalter retained its direct link with Christ Church Priory (and after the Reformation the Dean and Chapter).

The products of this area - salt, fish and oysters - would have been valuable contributions to the great monastic institution at Canterbury and to local trade. Quite possibly there were other vessels like the Graveney boat which had their individual hard standing places along the creeks and within easy reach of higher, drier, ground. Christ Church may well have favoured trade at Seasalter, on its own land, as the more usual route through the port of Fordwich on the Stour involved much conflict over rights and dues with its great rival, the Abbey of St Augustine.

What evidence is there, then, for the presence of an important Saxon settlement here at Seasalter based on this economic activity and wealth? One of the ancient creeks of the marshland skirted round the eastern edge of the higher ground and here today stands the church of St Alphege. Its position was once very significant for it is shown as a sea-mark on maps from the sixteenth century onward. The existing building, now reduced to the chancel, may date from the early twelfth century, though there are indications of an earlier structure[7]. Hasted in his 'History of Kent' also records another building: 'By the great storm, which happened on Jan.1,1779, there was discovered among the beach on the sea shore, at Codhams corner... the stone foundations of a large long building, lying due east and west, supposed to have been the remains of the ancient church of Seasalter'[8]. This location would be off today's Blue Anchor corner; whatever was revealed was again buried, so its significance remains a mystery. Tradition has it that this was the Saxon church which had to be abandoned as the sea advanced and the building was overwhelmed in a great storm.

Today landward of St Alphege there is a wide stretch of gently rising ground. Looking at the Tithe Map there are recorded here the names of 'Great Field' and 'Church Field', suggesting the layout of a medieval field system, generally regarded as originating in late Saxon times. Then there is an aerial photograph of this area taken during the very dry summer of1947 which revealed a group of crop marks which might indicate the site of a settlement[9]. Church Lane, which follows the edge of the higher ground (see map page 22), was the ancient way from Canterbury down to the coast at Blue Anchor corner, and was possibly of Roman origin as discussed in Chapter Two. At this point, near the coast today, a map of 1693 shows two large buildings: one probably a tithe barn (this being Rectory Field), and the other a substantial building called 'The Lookers House'[10]. The 'looker' was the herdsman who 'looked after' the livestock grazing on the marshes; for such a person one would have expected a simple cottage rather than a well

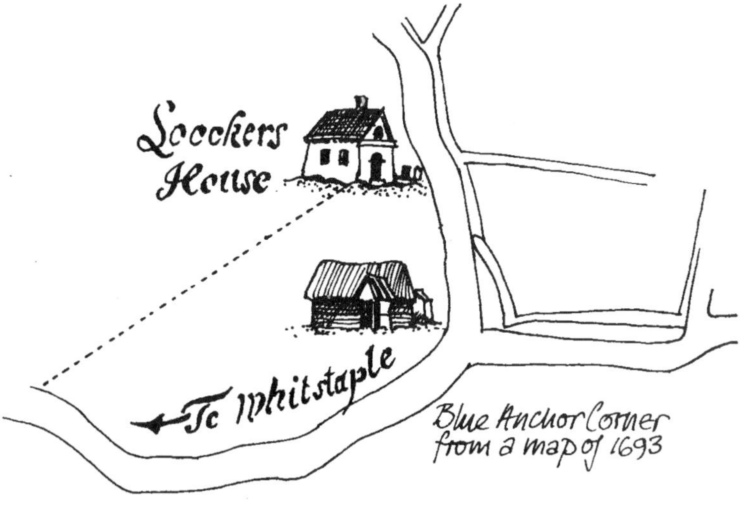

Blue Anchor Corner
from a map of 1693

constructed house. The shape of the building is somewhat reminiscent of a Saxon nave, such as at Bradwell-on-Sea in Essex, and a religious connection is suggested by the gravestone-like objects drawn by the entrance. Can this then be the 'St Elpheis Chappell' at 'Sesalterstrete' described as being by the shore hereabouts in 1481?[11] A chapel dating from the eleventh century would give some substance to the tradition that the body of Archbishop Alphege, murdered as a captive of the Danes in 1023, was returned to Canterbury partly by a sea journey and then landed at Seasalter[12]. This was an event which might have been piously commemorated by the building of a chapel. After the Reformation such a good sound building might well have been put to practical use as 'The Lookers House'.

The key to unravelling the early history of Seasalter lies in examining further the changing relationship between land and sea levels as shown in the diagram page 25[13]. As described in Chapter Two the dramatic nature of this process has been demonstrated by the discovery of the Graveney boat entombed under two metres of estuarine clay. Even the ground surface above lies well below Spring tide level. The historical record suggests that there have been periods of marked advance by the sea followed by periods of little change. Thus there appears to have been widespread use of the coastal area in Roman times well beyond the present shore. From the eleventh century many documents express growing concern about inundations: was it perhaps at this period that the building recorded by Hasted was destroyed? Problems reached a peak in the thirteenth century with accounts of disastrous flooding and the consequent loss of land, and always the records give graphic details of the accompanying tremendous storms[14].

The cause of these storm surges, as they are called, is now understood. An unusually deep depression to the north of Scotland sweeps vast quantities of water into the North Sea basin at a time of high Spring-tide level. Gale force winds then drive the waves onshore, battering the coastline and raising sea-level far above normal high tide level. Low-lying areas are overwhelmed and what the sea has then claimed it will endeavour to hold on to.

Against this attack sea defences are the only protection. Thus it was that in 1325 the Prior of Christ Church wrote to the Archbishop on behalf of his Seasalter tenants, proposing joint action to protect their lands by the building of an embankment[15]. The result was the construction of a substantial bank over a mile in length and forty feet broad. Initially this did not withstand battering by the sea and further work was needed to mend breaches.

The marshes were finally made secure in 1340, although maintaining these sea defences was a continuing process for gradually rising sea level required them to be strengthened and raised. Behind, various improvements were made to the drainage of the marshes, with the present pattern of straight dykes dating from the sixteenth century. Mr Boulting at work on the Hammond Drain was continuing this tradition.

Even in our own times the continuing vulnerability of these lands has been apparent. For in the early hours of 1st February 1953 a storm surge gathered strength and attacked down the whole coastline of eastern England[16]. At Seasalter the fury of the waves tore a fifty foot gap in the sea wall near the Sportsman Inn, water poured through and fanned out in all directions to flood the whole of the marshes. As daylight came a terrible sight was revealed: *'Here and there the carcases of animals could be seen - many more lay hidden under the still, sinister surface of the water. It is estimated that hundreds of sheep and cattle have been drowned; only when the water subsides will the true figures be known.' As RSPCA Inspector Miles recounted 'The wind was so fierce that two local men and he could make no headway in their boat. They saw the animals disappear one by one. They did, however, manage to get a number of others to the safety of the railway embankment. The most pathetic case was that of two bulllocks seen standing on the carcases of five others. Mr Creed tried to get them to the railway, but on the way they fell down in only a foot of water and died from exhaustion.'*[17]

The battering by the waves destroyed the beach huts lining the sea wall, in some cases hurling them bodily on to the road the other side; the flood waters swirled round to Seasalter Cross, inundating houses and chalets; inland the waters reached up and over the railway line to the southern edge of the Seasalter Levels. So for several weeks a new bay of the sea had been created, and once again transport was by boat.

References

1. Fenwick V, '**The Graveney Boat**', National Maritime Museum Archaeological Series No 3, BAR British Series 53 1978.
2. Evans JH '**Archaeological horizons in the north Kent marshes**', AC v. LXVI, 1953, p.103.
3. Witney KP, 'The **Development of the Kent Marshes**', AC v. CVII, 1989 p.29.
4. Ward G, 'The **Origins of Whitstable**', AC v. LVII, 1944, pp.51-55. (Note: his identification with 'Dodeham' in Domesday Book is not accepted.)

Later **salt production** in the thirteenth century produced conspicuous mounds on the Levels: see Thompson MW, '**A Group of Mounds on Seasalter Level, near Whitstable and the Medieval embanking in this area**', AC v. LXX, 1956 p.44.

5. Morgan P, ed. '**The Domesday Book of Kent**', Phillimore, 1983.
6. Drewett P, Rudling D and Gardiner M, '**The South-East to AD1000**' Longman 1988 pp. 336-37.
   Baldwin R, '**Seasalter: a problem borough in Domesday Kent** re-examined', AC v. CX 1992 p.237. (Note: an important study with wide-ranging sources and a very full Bibliography; but the conclusion, identifying Saxon Seasalter with the site of Whitstable is not accepted here. See Chapter Four 'The Borough of Harwich').
7. Porter B, '**Seasalter Domesday borough**', brief guide, Canterbury Council 1987.
8. **Hasted** E 'The History and Topographical Survey of the County of Kent' 2nd ed. 1797-1800, reprinted EP Publishing Ltd 1972, v. VIII, p.103.
9. WT 18.1.1990 photograph.
10. 'A Mapp & Perfect Description of Several pieces of Land lying in the Parish of Seasalter... by Thomas Bourne 1693', copy Whitstable Museum: Wallace Harvey collection.
11. Thompson MW, ref 4. above, p.66.
    In our preceding book - Pike, Page and Cann, 'Ales and Tales' p.16 the identification with St Peter's Chapel is withdrawn and the link with St Elpheis preferred.
12. Goodsall RH ref. 5. above, p.72. Also Baldwin R ref. 6. above, p.255.
13. Information from Thompson ref. 4. above p.49; and Fenwick ref. 1. above pp.165-6.
14. Bowler E, 'A **History of Coast Protection in the Whitstable Area**', report to Canterbury City Council (n/d), Whitstable Museum, Wallace Harvey collection.
15. Thompson MW, ref. 4. above p.47.
16. For the effects of this and **earlier floods** on the town of Whitstable, see Pike, Page and Cann 'Ales and Tales', Whitstable Improvement Trust 1993, chapter 8, 'The Fight against the Sea'.
    Summers D, 'The East Coast Floods', David and Charles 1978.
17. WT 7.2.53, 14.2.53.

4 THE TOWER OF ALL SAINTS CHURCH

Today the tower of All Saints church seems unremarkable, set among the trees of the churchyard and attached to the nave of quite a large parish church. Only from the top is it possible to appreciate the splendid panorama which confirms its hill-top location. On a clear day to the south the wooded scarp of the Blean stands out; northwards across the estuary can be glimpsed the distant coast of Essex; eastwards lies Reculver and to the west the Swale and beyond it the Isle of Sheppey.

Charts of the coastline from the sixteenth century, with their sketches of the church as a distinctive feature, and its use in navigational bearings for sailors and the fixing of local boundaries, indicate it importance as a seamark. This significance is also illustrated in old documents, as in this example from 1671 when the Court of Fishing defined the limits of working on the oyster ground:

'The fishing begins eastward from an oak called Scotts Oak in Clowes Wood upon Rayham Trees - in the Stream so far off as Blackbournes House a sails breadth in Shelness in Sheppey - and as far West in the same stream as Scotts Oak upon Whitstable Church.'[1]

View of 'Frankpledge' gathering
at All Saints Tower.

Like many prominent features easily seen from offshore the church tower was white-washed each year with a grant from the Brethren of Trinity House who looked after all kinds of navigational aids for seamen. This custom was only discontinued in 1875 when the building underwent extensive restoration[2]. The structure of the tower suggests some special function beyond its religious one. It is relatively large: 52 feet high, with stout walls of rubble, stones and flints. Inside is an ancient stairway composed of massive timbers made from diagonally split and roughly squared logs, probably original to its construction, which architectural features suggest as the thirteenth century. The body of the existing church was built at least a century later.

The tower has supporting buttresses on each side including one on the inside of the church; this has clearly been cut down from a height matching the others. If the tower had been built integral with and supported by a nave, then such a buttress would not have been required. The inference must be therefore that the tower was originally free-standing. During the restoration work fragments of carved stonework and a font were found imbedded in the church walls: these must have formed part of an earlier structure, perhaps of the twelfth century - indeed the rudely carved font might even have had a Saxon origin. Evidence from excavations at other churches suggest that such an early church would have been a very small building[3]. So when built the massive tower would have appeared an even more distinctive feature, set up on its hill and visible from considerable distances both from the countryside and from out at sea.

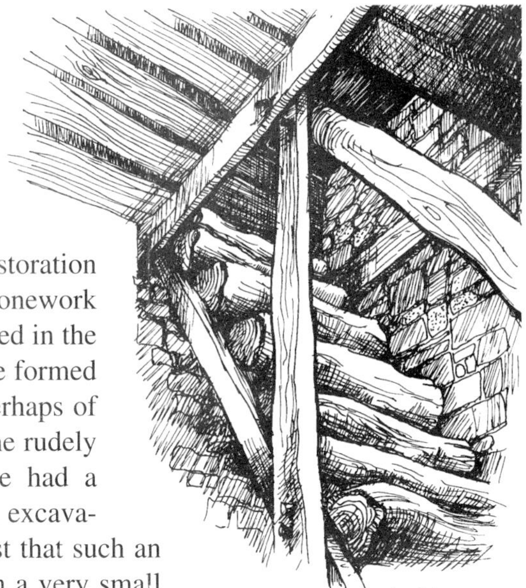
Ancient stairway - All Saints Church.

Evidence from the Domesday Book

Another clue to the significance of this ancient church tower is to be found in the details of that massive survey of the land undertaken on the orders of the conquering William of Normandy, which became known as the Domesday Book. The Anglo-Saxon Chronicle records that about New Year's Day, 1086:

'... the king had much thought and very deep discussion with his council about this country - how it was settled, and with what kind of people. Then he sent his men over all England, into every shire, and had them find out how many hundred hides there were in the shire, or what land or cattle the king himself had in the country, or what dues he ought to have each year from the shire. Also he had a record made of how much land his archbishops had, and his bishops, abbots and earls - and though I relate at too great length - what or how much everybody had who was occupying land in England, in land or livestock, and how much money it was worth. So very strictly did he have it

investigated that there was no single hide nor a yard of land, nor indeed... one ox nor one cow nor one pig was left out, and not put down in his record: and afterwards all these writings were brought to him'.[4]

This was a vast undertaking with the Commissioners crossing the land, questioning, recording and checking to produce a unique document: 'No other country in the world possesses such a detailed record from so far back in time.' This compilation was needed by King William in order to rule his kingdom effectively; to know who held the land and therefore owed him allegiance; to estimate the value of each holding and so its potential for taxation; and by implication it recorded the whole structure of society from the slave and the poorest peasant to the greatest barons - all were accounted for. So definitive was the survey regarded that it soon became known as the 'Domesday' - the 'Day of Judgment'.

The Domesday Book is therefore a tremendous source of information, to be used, however, with two provisos: it was not devised as a gazeteer - for example numerous villages known to have existed at the time are not recorded - and secondly, the detailed information was not undertaken with the consistency of modern statistical surveys - there is scope to interpret and to disagree.

For the local area there are entries clearly identifiable for the landholding at Seasalter (recorded as Seseltre) and Swalecliffe (Soanclive). Between these, where lies the old town of Whitstable, scholars agree that the land is described under the designation 'Nortone', meaning 'Northwood'[5]. In early Saxon days this word was used very widely for the country lying to the north of the Blean Forest, but by 1086 settlements had become established with individual names and the old term remained attached to this particular area. As we shall see later, it remained in use as late as the sixteenth century[6].

Whitstable: the origin of the name.

The name 'Witenestaple' - clearly an early form of Whitstable - does, however, appear in the Domesday record, but it is not the name of a manor, that is, a landholding, but refers to a much larger administrative unit of local jurisdiction and taxation: the Hundred. Place name experts interpret this word Witenestaple as deriving from the Early English 'hwitan stapole' which means a white pillar or post[7]. This is very plausible, for many Hundreds took their names from some prominent feature in the locality for a reason shortly to be discussed. Now a white pillar or post certainly suggests a sea-mark and this might well have been a predecessor of the white-washed church tower of All Saints' which had this function in later centuries.

Broadly, the Hundred of Whitstable comprised the area of the parishes of Whitstable, Blean and Swalecliffe[8]. Medieval boundaries were not, of course, in a modern sense, lines laid out on a map; they evolved through the expansion of communities as new land was taken into cultivation. Boundaries were defined by the holding of land and the allegiance which this demanded, and might include elements stretching back over hundreds of years. Today their irregularities and anomalies seem very odd, but at the time people locally knew clearly the authority they must acknowledge. So we may define the Whitstable Hundred at the time of Domesday as a block of country stretching inland from the coast: to the west was the parish of Seasalter, a separate entity called a Liberty, and to the east the Hundred of Blengate (later absorbing part of Swalecliffe parish). Across the woods the Hundred included the lands around Blean, here having a clear physical boundary in the little Sarre Penn valley (now by the Red Lion public house). Beyond this, to the south, was the Hundred of Westgate which extended to the edge of the City of Canterbury.

The system of dividing the Shires - the Counties - into Hundreds was developed by the Saxons during the tenth century. In the kingdom of Kent, however, much larger units called Lathes had already been established. Whitstable was part of the Lathe of St Augustine which included the whole of the north-east of Kent. So the creation of Hundreds here was probably only under way at the time of the Conquest and was then completed by the Normans, in order to have a uniform system of administration[9].

It is thought that the Hundred originated from the basis on which it was organised: approximately one hundred 'hides' or 'carucates': these were measures of cultivated land (each reckoned to be some 200 acres[10]). This broad economic arrangement reflected the role of the Hundred in the system of taxation. It also played a major role in the King's control of the great mass of the peasantry: a means of demonstrating his authority, maintaining order and dispensing justice.

This control was exercised through a remarkable system of collective responsibility which, like the Hundred, the invading Normans took over from their Saxon predecessors and extended as a means of containing and controlling a rebellious, defeated people. The peasantry were, then, organised in groups of ten or perhaps twelve men - all males over the age of twelve were included - and grouped on a local basis so that they could act together. This group was called a tithing[11]. These men were mainly the 'unfree' peasants, the villeins, who were bound in service to their lord; in return for work on his land - the 'demesne' - they received their own holding on which to subsist.

Checking that all the men were accounted for in a tithing was the responsibility of the Sheriff of the Shire who would visit each Hundred twice yearly to receive the report of his representative, the Bailiff. The men of each tithing were mutually responsible for their own good behaviour and respect for the law and local custom. For example, anyone observing a felony being committed was required under 'Hue and Cry' to call out his neighbours to join the 'hue' and help arrest the wrong-doer. Then the tithing was responsible for ensuring that the accused person duly appeared for trial and for presenting the necessary evidence.

Each tithing had a head-man, usually elected by the men, who bore the main responsibility for the group; any failure to discharge their duties would result in a fine, and possibly the confiscation of goods. In Kent, the tithings were known as 'borgs' and the leader as the 'borsholder'. The twice-yearly visit of the Sheriff was called the 'View of Frankpledge'. At this gathering of all the tithings a jury of twelve would be empanelled to hear complaints concerning misdemeanours, infringements of local customs, and to adjudicate on personal disputes. These 'presentments' were made by the borsholders, or 'chief pledges' as they were called, since they were pledged or bound to to see that all the accused were present to answer the charges brought against them.

These presentments might include accusations of brawls and disorderly behaviour; failure to maintain local bridges and highways; complaints of nuisances such as undrained ditches, obstructed pathways and polluted wells or springs; breaches of the regulations governing the prices and measures and quality of ale and bread. Understandably the View was alternatively called the 'law day': it was principally held in the autumn when after the gathering of the harvest the peasants had resources to meet any fines imposed. Considerable revenue could result from the View. Not only did it therefore render all the peasantry of the Hundred accountable, but in addition they were required to make a payment, nominally for the costs of holding the View, but in effect a local tax.

For this gathering together of a large body of men there would not have been a building large enough to accommodate them; as we have seen such churches as existed were very small. The assembly would therefore have been held in the open air at some prominent and easily accessible point in the Hundred. From the derivation of the name 'Witenestaple' we know that the local assembly was at the 'white pillar or post' and this may be identified with the location of 'Church-hill', as the situation of all Saints Church was referred to in the seventeenth century. Indeed what would have been more natural, when the Church began to establish its own authority, than to build at an existing point of assembly? And, in due course, to add an impressive tower to their small church, both to act as a symbol for the faithful, and also as a very effective replacement for the ancient wooden or stone marker?

There is now an important conclusion to make at this point concerning the place we call Whitstable today: in 1086 and for some centuries following this area formed the manor of Northwood. Any reference to Whitstable in the great variety of spellings then encountered, applies to that much larger area of the Hundred which stretched southward to include Blean.

'Northwood':the medieval manor.

The Domesday Book recorded that the manor of Northwood was then held by Lanfranc, the first Norman Archbishop[12]. It comprised thirteen sulungs; at the estimated one sulung to 200 acres: this gives a total of 2000 acres. On this there was land for 26 ploughs (again a measure of land), and for the lord on his own land - the demesne - a further two ploughs. There were ten acres of meadow and woodland sufficient for 50 pigs. There were 92 villagers with 40 of them smallholders, having 59½ ploughs. A church is recorded.

The total value of this manor before 1066 was £24.5s.0d; later as much; at Domesday it paid £50.14.2d to the Archbishop and 20s to the Archdeacon.

Within the lordship of Northwood there was also a separate holding by a sub-tenant, Vitalis. He had three sulungs one yoke and twelve acres; reckoning a yoke at 50 acres, this totals a further 662 acres. There was land for five ploughs and 'a small pig pasture of woodland'. Vitalis had 29 smallholders and five slaves. There were recorded seven 'salthouses' (that is saltworks) and also a church. The total value of this holding was £14.6.6 and as there is no reference to a pre-Conquest value, this was an estate of a more recent creation.

The relatively large size of the manor of Northwood is surprising, but it is partly explained by the fact that some of the lands held by Vitalis were actually at Sarre and Stourmouth[13].

As noted earlier Domesday was essentially a record of ownership and not a gazeteer. This separate land may certainly explain some of the six salt-works recorded, for the coast of the Wantsum channel (still open at this time) was particularly suitable for producing salt. There were local marshes which could have been very suitable also[14].

The large acreage of the manor of Northwood and the doubling in its value from pre-Conquest times would suggest quite intensive utilisation of the resources of the land; a policy very much promoted by Archbishop Lanfranc on his estates. Of growing importance were the coastal marshes as, in addition to salt production, they formed excellent pasture for sheep. These were put out from the first flush of Spring grass until early August when the sheep had been sheared and the ewes weaned. 'They gave meat when culled or superannuated, with parchment from their skins, their droppings were the best and most plentiful form of fertilizer; their treading improved the texture of the soil instead of puddling it; and their close cropping helped to eliminate weeds.'[15]

On the death of Lanfranc in 1089 the lordship must have reverted to the Crown for it was subsequently granted to Fulbert de Lacy who held the Barony of Chilham and took the surname 'de Dover'[16]. It then descended through branches of this family: in 1250, for example, the manor of Northewode was held by Richard de Dover. A list of Kentish knights of this period shows that the sub-tenant was one Willelmus de Wiltone, and 'Whitestaple' is given as an alternative name for the holding. A second sub-manor is also recorded, for Johannes de Cundeshalle held lands from Willelmo Lungespeye, himself a tenant of the Bishop of Lincoln[17]. The story of this manor - Cundes Hall - is dealt with more extensively in Chapter Five.

Indeed, by this time, with the growth of the practice of holding land by rent, and the marked expansion of population, it is probable that the original Northwood land had become divided between sub-manors and farms[18].

The Manor and the mystery of 'Graystone'.

When the son of Richard de Dover died without an heir the manor passed to his sister Isobel and was held by her husband Alexander de Baliol during his lifetime on behalf of her infant son John, Earl of Athol (the title coming from her first husband). In 1293 de Baliol was required to appear before the King's Justices to justify his claims to lands and rights which he then held; these included 'free warren, gallows, wreck of the sea and waif in Whitstable'. He stated further that 'he held the Manor of Whitstable and the Hundred of Whitstable by the law of England, of the inheritance of John, Earl of Athol, by reason which he claimed to have in the same hundred which the aforesaid manor is, view of frankpledge, amendment of the assize of bread and ale, infang, thief and gallows, and waifs'[19].

He also presented a further claim which raises a mystery: 'toll with merchandise at le Craston in the same manor'. The name appears later as Greston and then Greystone or Graystone. So where could this landing place have been situated? The same claim is made in 1312 by the following lord, Bartholomew de Badlesmere. In support of his claim the jury made reference to precedent: namely that a boat cast up on 'the Graystone in Whitstable' had been taken by de Baliol properly exercising his right as Lord of the Manor[20]. Then there is a reference to Graystone in 1326, when the King ordered some local knights to be responsible for searching vessels along the north Kent coast for subversive letters being smuggled in from abroad. This duty was allocated in three sections: Graystone to Faversham, Reculver to Graystone, and at the 'Vills' of Whitstable and Faversham (the last being presumably points where more boats landed). The writ was repeated the following year, again referring to the 'coast of the Thames, between Reculver, Graystone and Whitstable'[21]. Clearly this Graystone was a place separate from Whitstable and a landing place of some significance at this time.

The use of the word 'vill' in this document and its linking with Faversham (then undoubtedly a town) raises the question of whether it has the same implication for Whitstable. Unfortunately terms like this were not used with such strict accuracy. It certainly suggests that there was now a specific 'place' known as 'Whitstable' (that is distinct from the Hundred) but it does not imply an organised settlement as distinct from a scattering of fishermen's huts along the shore.

This landing place, Graystone, was still in use in 1426-27, for Cathedral accounts record 80 tons of Merstham stone from Battersea being brought for the rebuilding of the south-west tower: 'And paid to William Stephens for water carriage of the same to Greyston at 16p per ton £5.6.8d. and for carrying the same from Greyston to Canterbury at 16d per ton, £4.'[22]. The

Stephens family were prominent land and boat owners who lived near All Saints Church. The same landing place may have been used in 1483 when the city accounts record that 'ashlar stone was brought from Maidstone to Whitstable and then overland to the city.'[23]

There is even a later reference to Greystone in a dispute of 1585 concerning the organisation of the 'Watch' maintaining a beacon at Denge Marsh on the south coast. In support of their case the protesting men cited an earlier and, they claimed, an identical situation which had operated along the north coast of Kent. And among the watch places they named 'Greiston' where twelve men should be responsible. However the authenticity of this record was challenged 'being written in a spare leaf, at the latter end of the same booke, and may for that cause be thought rather to be some tale or heresie otherwise.'[24] So we cannot regard Graystone as an important watch and beacon point, or that it was still in existence as late as 1585.

What then do we know about Graystone? Clearly it lay off the present coastline for this has receded since that time. It was located to the east of Whitstable and the 'greystone' formed a sufficient obstruction to wreck a ship. It provided a 'hard' or quay where ships could load and unload; there must have been firm access to the shore linking with an easy and established route to Canterbury in order to transport heavy stone. Its development may have been a deliberate policy by one of the Lords of the Manor in order to gain dues from vessels using Graystone. Its disappearance from the historical record was most probably the result of the gradual retreat of the coastline: it may have been overwhelmed by one of the storms which have afflicted this area. So today we must search for Graystone out under the sea.

The first obvious candidate for its location would be off the end of that extraordinary shingle ridge at Tankerton, The Street or 'Street of Stones' as it was earlier known. This long pebbly feature has very much the character of a trackway today, stretching away at the lowest tide for a distance of three quarters of a mile. It is however a purely natural occurrence produced by a more resistant layer in the London clay which has collected a covering of shingle and shells due to tidal action. At the turn of the century photographs show that it was then further east, much broader and uneven in its surface. The Oyster Map of 1770 marks it very clearly with banks of stones at the seaward end, but it also shows a narrow channel between its end and the shore. There is a local fishermen's tradition that the remains of buildings have been seen off the end of the Street and they used to refer to the waters

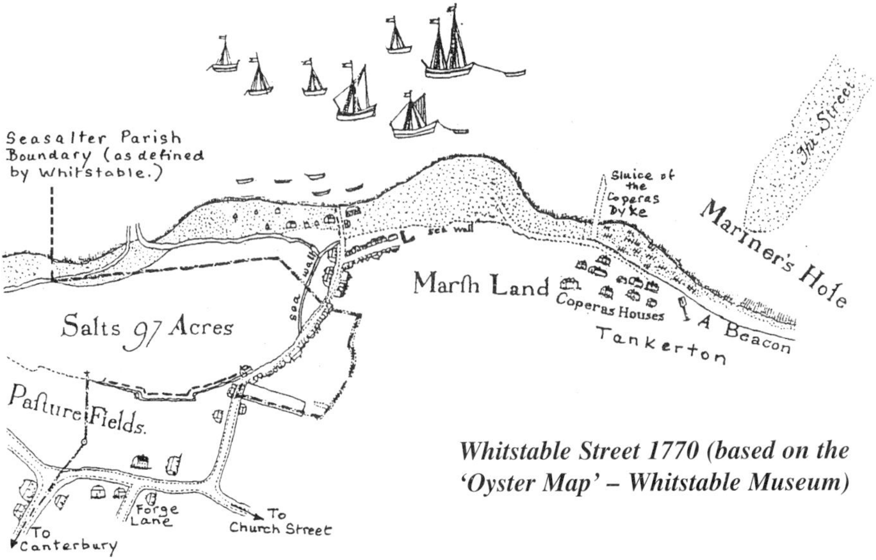

Whitstable Street 1770 (based on the 'Oyster Map' – Whitstable Museum)

nearby as the Grayes[25]. One of the ancient routes across the Blean to the coast came to Tankerton: in 1488 there is a reference to the mending of 'the Canterbury Way leading to Tankerton.'[26] There are, of course, steep cliffs along the coast here but this disadvantage could have been overcome as later, at the time of the copperas works here, their trackway sloped down at an angle to the quays below. Indeed, did the existence of an earlier landing point in this vicinity lead to the siting of the copperas works at Tankerton? There is a detailed account of this little industrial area in Chapter Eight.

A second possible location for Graystone would be further to the east off Long Rock at Swalecliffe (illustration p 10). Here again there is a more solid base in the London clay which probably extends for a considerable distance seaward, for there has been a significant retreat of the coastline here, as discussed in Chapter One. It is known that the stream, the Swale Brook, originally had a more northerly course and crossing the wide foreshore it would have provided a suitable creek for boats to use with one or more 'hards' on the side, as we have seen with the Saxon Graveney boat in Chapter Three.

In this area. too, there was a point where one of the ancient routes from Canterbury, crossing the Blean Forest, reached the coast: it is referred to in a charter of AD948: '...the high road which runs from Canterbury to Swalecliffe...'[27].

Some years ago movement of the beach material after a storm revealed the remains of a wrecked boat in this vicinity and pottery recovered suggested a sixteenth century date. A similar circumstance in 1953 brought to light a gold Merovingian coin of the seventh century[28]. This is an area which certainly warrants detailed investigation both for its archaeology as we have seen earlier in Chapter One, and also as a possible location for the landing point of Graystone. But for the moment the question of its location remains unanswered.

The Whitstable Market - in Canterbury.

In 1312 Bartholomew de Badlesmere 'was summoned to answer to the Lord the King on the plea of: by which warrant he claims to have [rights] in his Manor of Chilham...' and this included the manor of Whitstable. The claims made by de Baliol are repeated, including 'tollage of merchandize at la Greyston' and there was also a claim to a further right which this time presents no mystery, for it can be traced across the centuries to the present day: 'the claim to have a certain liberty in the Town of Canterbury pertaining to his Manor of Whitstable that all his tenants being fishermen shall have a certain place in the High Street between the Church of All Saints and the Church of St Andrew containing in length fourscore feet and in breadth three feet for selling their fish without giving toll to anyone.'[29]

So valuable did the city regard the fish trade from Whitstable that in 1480 they moved the market to a paved area near St Margaret's Church and later provided a market building there. Although this also then contained the City's fish market, the Whitstable section was separate and its toll free right maintained. In 1822 the old Tudor building was pulled down and replaced with one in the fashionable classical style, but it still retained the old name of the 'Whitstable Market'. The Greek pedimented front remains in St Margarets Street today, though no longer a place selling fish. This building therefore illustrates a remarkable historical continuity, linking Whitstable to Canterbury.

The 'Borough of Harwich': an historical puzzle.

The small stone at the foot of Whitstable's War Memorial in the library forecourt appears an insignificant reminder of the past, yet it does provide a clue to a curious feature of the town. On the south side of the stone are the letters 'WP', indicating the parish of Whitstable, and on the other the letters 'SP' show that of Seasalter. It marks the boundary line between these two.

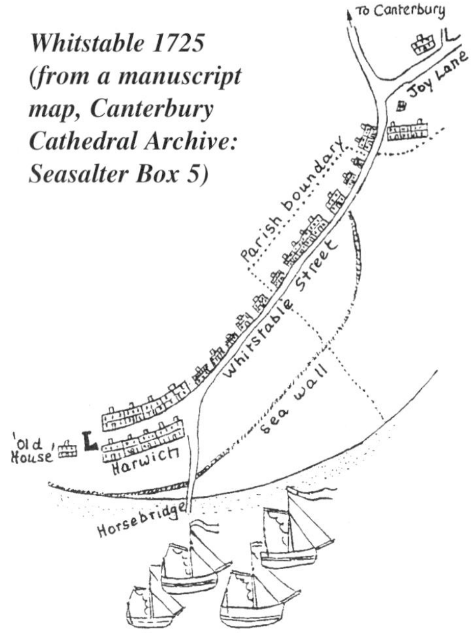

Whitstable 1725 (from a manuscript map, Canterbury Cathedral Archive: Seasalter Box 5)

What is unusual is the way this boundary swings round to the east and then recrosses the main street by Gladstone Road. The town is therefore split between these two parishes. Today this is of no significance but up to the end of the nineteenth century many aspects of local administration were organised on a parish basis and so this division resulted in many anomalies in the affairs of the town.

The map of 1725 shows that the original settlement from which Whitstable has grown is represented today by the wide western end of Harbour Street: it was a tiny fishing village. As the maritime trade grew the little community expanded with houses being built along the highway to Canterbury, a story which forms the subject of Chapter Six. This long straggling place then became appropriately known as 'Whitstable Street'. So this was not a town which parish boundaries then divided, but a small settlement which gradually grew from its own parish into the adjacent one.

As we saw earlier the local parishes were contained within the larger medieval areas of the Liberty of Seasalter and the Hundred of Whitstable. But here is another historical puzzle: the early inhabitants of the land which ultimately formed the town of Whitstable belonged to neither the Liberty nor the Hundred but were instead part of the Hundred of Westgate which lay on the north side of the City of Canterbury. They lived in what was called the 'Borough of Harwich'.

The 'Borough' was made up of three separate parts as shown on the map, designated as being in Tankerton, in Seasalter and in Northwood[30]. The word 'borough' is not to be confused with the usual meaning of an urban settlement; in Kent it was also used, as here, for a sub-division of the Hundred and perhaps derived from the borgh unit of the Frankpledge system which was described earlier[31].

Detached portions of Hundreds and parishes were actually quite common,

The Borough of Harwich

1. Northwood
2. Seasalter
3. Tankerton

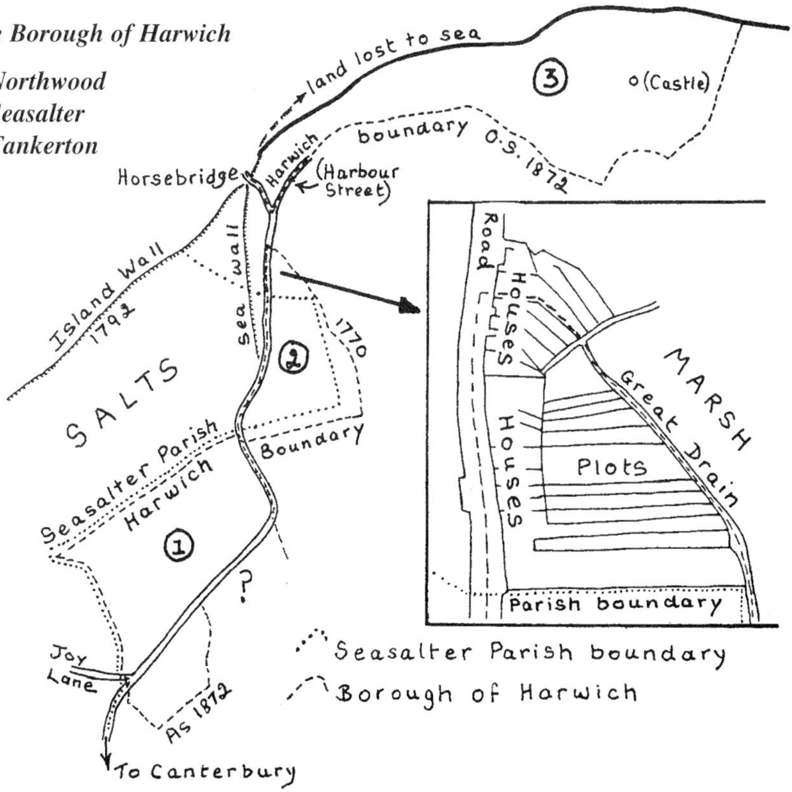

making the mapping of medieval boundaries today exceedingly complicated. Nearly always they originated for practical economic reasons, giving access to resources which the community lacked in their main area. Self-sufficiency was the need in those earlier times. In Kent such detached areas occurred frequently in the marshland, providing as we have seen sheep pasture, salt-works and fishing; others were located in the heath and woodlands giving 'pannage' for pigs and the trees giving timber and charcoal.

What then might explain the origin of the Borough of Harwich and its connection with Westgate and its lord, the Archbishop? The location of the three sections, running along the 'Salts' and in Tankerton stretching along the coast, obviously suggests some maritime connection.

The clue would seem to lie in some Saxon charters[32]. In AD803 King Ethelbert made a grant of 'one salt evaporator, a salt works and its cottage at Herewic, and the leading of four carts in the Kings Wood for 6 weeks in the Kings Commoning'. And again in AD946 King Eadred granted land in Swalecliffe to Heresige, together with 'the wood clearing that there belongs and the saltworks at Herewic'. The similarity of the names Herewic and Harwich would suggest that they are the same place. So that valuable commodity, salt, would seem to be the answer to the origin of Harwich. The 'wic' ending occurs frequently, indicating places of some special function and which usually produced special tolls or taxes: salt making was one of these - in the Midlands are Droitwich and Nantwich, for example.

These Harwich saltworks may be some of those recorded in Domesday Book under 'Northwood' manor which, at this time, came within the lordship of the Archbishop, as did the Hundred of Westgate. Perhaps when the manor was returned to the Crown on the death of Lanfranc, the valuable salt-producing area was retained. The Archbishop in those days maintained a large establishment at his palace in Canterbury, and salt was essential for preserving fish and meat to last through the winter months. The separate sections named 'Seasalter' and 'Northwood' would indicate that these adjacent manors also had 'salt rights' in Harwich.

Thc boundary of the Borough of Harwich in Tankerton is particularly interesting: it includes the block of high ground in the east and then runs along the coast virtually to the edge of Seasalter parish. This would appear to cut off the people of Whitstable Hundred from the sea - so how did they obtain their fish to sell in Canterbury? Odd as it may seem, the manor/Hundred of Whitstable included the very wide foreshore (far beyond that of today) and also the stretch of water known as the 'Shallows' which formed the oyster ground: a very important right known as the 'Royalty of Fishing'. The Whitstable fisherfolk therefore would have lived out on the foreshore: the map of 1770 (see map p 42) shows that even at this much later time there was a significant number of buildings in this position. And indeed the description of the oyster industry, published in 1859 in Charles Dickens' magazine 'All the Year Round', describes the dredgermen as living in 'low, pitch-black wooden houses on the beach.'[34]

A very curious feature of this Tankerton boundary is that it runs along the middle of Harbour Street. So the north side, which certainly contains the oldest surviving buildings, and which must have formed the original fishing hamlet, actually lay in the Borough of Harwich. On the map of 1770 the letter 'L' is placed at the east end of this little street and it is described in the key as the 'east end of Harwich'. So these points would suggest that the original settlement was actually called 'Harwich' and then as it expanded along the roadway towards Canterbury it became known, in the eighteenth century, as 'Whitstable Street'[33].

The map of 1725 (page 44) illustrates a curious feature of the growth of the original settlement. There are buildings only along the east side of the roadway towards Canterbury. This cannot be due to any vulnerability of the west side to flooding, for it was protected by the Middle Wall. A reason appears when one notices that the boundary of the Borough of Harwich actually runs down the road; so only the east side is within Harwich. Then when the property boundaries in this part of Harwich are examined on the Tithe Map of 1842 the regularity in their layout clearly indicates some degree of planned layout, which finishes at the large drain protecting the plots from the marshland beyond (map p. 45).

This suggestion of planning is supported by a walk along the Borough section of the High Street today: it is easy to recognise that three quite substantial brick properties, Nos 73, 79 and 83, probably of late sixteenth century date, are virtually identical in appearance. So it would appear that Whitstable Street did not grow haphazardly: its development was planned by creating plots contained within the Archbishop's land - the Borough of Harwich. This is yet another aspect of Whitstable which awaits further investigation: doubtless the answer is buried deep in the Cathedral Archive.

From the sixteenth century: rights and lands.

We must now return to consider briefly the later history of the Manor of Whitstable[35]. King Richard II granted the lordship to his uncle Thomas Woodstock, Duke of Gloucester. In 1393 he decided to establish a religious foundation, the College of Pleshey, in Essex, and as part of the endowment he gave his rights at Whitstable. And so the manor remained with the College until it was suppressed by Henry VIII at the Reformation and reverted to the Crown. In 1546 its rights and privileges were defined:

'Why Staple is a hundred and keeps the court every three weeks - the Leyght (Leet) twice in the year and the Law Day once - the wrecks of the Sea are the Lords. The tenants have the fishing in the Shallow here paying a rent to the Lord for the same. All the Lordships is his Lords Free Warren both for Fowl and Wild Beasts. The Royal Fishery is the Lords.'[36]

By this time the ancient View of Frankpledge at the Law Day had become no more than a formality with the law-money being paid as an annual due to his lordship. Practical affairs were dealt with now, as elsewhere, by the manorial courts: the Court Baron (presumably meeting frequently) which dealt with matters concerning the management of the land, and the Court Leet (meeting twice yearly) which dealt with misdemeanours and minor offences. Within the Hundred the law was upheld by Constables appointed from within the community and most offences and serious crimes were dealt with by the local Justices.

In 1573 the manor yet again having reverted to the Crown Queen Elizabeth granted it to three men for their loyal services: Thomas Hennage, Michael Hennage and Moyle Finch[37]. It was then described as 'our manor of old called Norwood and now called St Annes and Court leys... and all to Court Leet appertaining...' This new designation is interesting for St Anne's must refer to the block of land around St Anne's Well at Tankerton. There was a religious foundation here: around AD 1500 references occur to the 'Brotherhood of St Anne' and the 'Hermyghe of St Anne'[38]. Presumably this religious community must have been situated at the place which later became the farm St Anne's Barn. Religious sites connected with wells and springs were quite common in Kent and are thought to have had their origin in the pagan Celtic (that is pre-Roman) period. So St Anne's may have been a survival from that early period of local history. The 'hermitage' and the surrounding land must again have been confiscated by Henry VIII in his suppression of religious institutions.

The manor of Whitstable subsequently passed, in effect now by sale, through several aristocratic families until in the late eighteenth century it was part of the estates of Lord Bolingbroke. In 1791 he was obliged to sell his manorial rights and lands at Whitstable to redeem family debts. This was a major event in determining the later history of the town[39].

The Manor and the modern town.

To the west of the village of the late eighteenth century (as shown on the map of 1770) were the 'Salts' of 97 acres of saltmarsh. This was purchased by three local men: John Nutt, Stephen Salisbury, and Edward Foad. They now excluded the sea by building along the shingle banks and closing the gap between - thus creating the Island Wall. This enabled the rapidly growing town to expand on its western side and Island Wall was to become the centre of the boat repairing and building industry (see Chapter Nine).

The 'Royalty of Fishing or Oyster Drudging' was purchased by a group of the Oyster Freemen who had previously paid rent to the lordship. After a complicated legal process that involved obtaining a special Act of Parliament they established in 1793 the 'Whitstable Company of Free Fishers and Dredgers' which, over the next fifty years, became the most important oyster industry in the country, making Whitstable's name virtually synonymous with oysters'.

The title 'Lord of the Manor' was bought, together with the St Anne's Farm at Tankerton, by Charles Pearson, a London businessman. He began the building of a residence which became the first part of Tankerton Castle. Through him and the subsequent owners of the estate the land at Tankerton remained undeveloped until 1890 when a new seaside resort was planned and launched. The story of these later events is told in Chapter Eight.

The traditional Court Leet was continued by Charles Pearson and the subsequent owners of the Castle. For a time entries were still made in the Court Roll as a means of registering changes in the ownership of land, but later, holding the court meant no more than attending a good dinner at the Bear and Key Hotel. The last occupant of the Castle, Mr Albert Mallandain, held the last one in the 1920s, so bringing to an end the last vestige of the historic Manor of Whitstable.

In the churchyard of All Saints, close by the tower with which this chapter opened, there is a large mausoleum built by Wynn Ellis, Lord of the Manor in mid-Victorian times. A London silk merchant, he had purchased the title, the Castle, and the surrounding land from the Pearsons. Wynn Ellis was a great entrepreneur and became a millionaire; he was for some years a Member of Parliament and held the office of Sheriff of Hertfordshire. A notable art collector, his bequest to the National Gallery provided some of its most valued pictures. His life and role in Whitstable are more fully explored in Chapter Eight; meantime we can observe that Wynn Ellis can stand comparison with some of the great aristocratic landowners and Men of State who also bore the title of Lord of the Manor of Whitstable.

References

1. Court of Fishing, 26 July 1671. From the '**Abstract of Ancient Records**' - relating to the Manor and Royalty of Whitstable transcribed for the Whitstable Company of Free Fishers and Dredgers by Joseph Burtt at the Public Record Office 1856-67, p.17.
Most of these records were printed in Appendix to the Case of the Free Fishers and Dredgers against John Foreman, at the Court of Common Pleas: 8.7.1867. Reference to this later as '**Legal Case**'.

These documents are in the records of the Oyster company; copies in the Wallace Harvey archive at Whitstable Museum.

2. Green IW, '**A History of All Saints**' Church', published by the Church, 2nd ed. 1970 (The ancient stonework has unfortunately disappeared.)
3. Brown Tim T, '**Churches in the Canterbury Diocese in the Eleventh Century**' in Blair J, 'Minsters and Parish Churches 950 - 1200 AD.' Oxford 1988.
   Philip B and Gough H, 'Early Church Discovered at Herne', Kent Archaeological Review, No 44, Summer 1976, p.86.
4. Wood M, '**Domesday** - A Search for the Roots of England', Book Club Associates for the BBC, 1987, quotation p.18, the comment following from the 'Introduction' p.10.
5. Morgan P, ed. '**Domesday Book: Kent**', Phillimore, Chichester 1983, 'Nortone' 2.14.
6. **Early Saxon settlement:**
   Brooks N, 'The **early history of the Church at Canterbury**', Leicester 1984, pp.100-106.
   'Abstract' ref 1. above, p.8: 'Our Manor of Whitstable of Old called Norwood', in grant made by Elizabeth I, 1573.
   The relationship of medieval settlement to local topography is discussed Chapter Five.
7. Wallenberg JK, '**Place Names of Kent**', Upsalla 1931, v.2 p.493.
   Anderson O, '**English Hundred Names**', Lund 1934, pp.148-49.

Both authorities give a wide variety of early spellings for the name 'Whitstable'.

8. **Whitstable Hundred** - the precise boundaries are impossible to determine: it would appear that there were changes over the centuries. The only map found is that in Hasted (see ref. 16 below) facing p 553. Approximately the Hundred of Whitstable comprised three parishes: Whitstable, Blean, and Swalecliffe. However Hasted in his heading for the chapter on 'Whitstaple' (p.505) records 'Whitstaple part of' but makes no comment in the text. On his map he includes the Broad Oak area of the parish of Hackington, ending in a point on the river Stour; no other mention of this inclusion has been found. Harris in his 'History of Kent' includes part of the parish of Nackington, to the south of Canterbury, in the Hundred and several other sources do this also. So has Hasted confused Hackington with Nackington? The eastern boundary runs through the parish of Swalecliffe, but Harris, for example, includes a part in the neighbouring Hundred of Blengate.
   In the early nineteenth century the Hundred was enlarged to include the parish of Seasalter.
   Only the Sarre Penn valley on the south side gave the Hundred a clear physical boundary.
9. Ward G, '**The Lathe** in Aylesford in 975', AC v. XLVI 1934, p.7.
10. This interpretation is generally agreed as in ref. 18 below.
11. The organisation of the **tithing and the View of Frankpledge** are discussed in most books on Medieval Society. The main complications and variations within the system are considered in Morris WA, 'The FrankpledgeSystem', Longmans Green and Co. 1910.
    For a short account and the later survival, see Keith-Lucas B, 'Parish Affairs: the Government of Kent under George III', Ch. IX 'The **Hundred and the Manor**'.
12. Morgan p, ref. 5 above.
13. Du Boulay, FR, 'The **Lordship of Canterbury**. An Essay on Medieval Society', London 1966. Appendix A pp.381-83.
14. On the east of the local area was the White Marsh (now Westmeads) and to the west, the 'Salts' (now largely the golf course), see the Map of 1770. For details of **medieval salt-making** see Thompson MW, 'A Group of Mounds on Seasalter Level, near Whitstable, and the Medieval Imbanking in this area', AC v. LXX 1956, p.44.
15. Witney KP, 'The **Development of the Kent Marshes** in the Aftermath of the Norman Conquest', AC v. CVII 1989 p.40.

16. For the **descent of the Manor of Whitstable** see:
Legal Case, ref. 1. above
Hasted, 'The History and topographical survey of the County of Kent', 2nd Ed. in 12 vols. 1797-1801, Edition EP Publishing Ltd 1972; 'The Hundred of Whitstable' v. VIII, p. 505.
Goodsall RH, 'Whitstable Seasalter and Swalecliffe - the History of Three Kent Parishes', Canterbury Chap 11 'The Middle Ages'.
17. Greenstreet J, '**Holders of Knight's fees in Kent**... anno 38 Henry III (1253-4)' AC v. XII, pp.204-5.
18. Miller, York CA, '**Society and economy in the Whitstable Hundred and Seasalter c1086-1525**' MA thesis No 3613, UKC 1992. Essentially a discussion of population estimates.
19. Legal Case ref 1. above p.21. (given as Placita de Warranto, Kent, 21 Ed I; M2/331) free warren - the right to kill game, waifs - right to seize abandoned goods or animals; infang, thief and gallows - right to hang thieves for offences committed on the manor and to seize their goods.
20. Legal Case ref. 1 above p.22 (given as Placita de Warranto, Kent 6 Edward II M2.34).
21. Legal Case ref. 1 above, pp.22-23 (given as Patent Roll, 19 Ed II pt 1 M7; and Close Roll, 20, Ed II M12.)
22. Woodruff CE, '**Rebuilding the South-west tower of Canterbury Cathedral** in the Fifteenth Century', AC v. XLV, 1933, p.45.
23. Brown Tim T, '**Report on St George's Gate**' for the Canterbury Archaeological Trust, AC v. CVI, 1988, p.159.
24. Lightfoot WJ, 'Documents relating to a Dispute between the 7 Hundreds and Lydd concerning the Watch at Denge Marsh, AC v. VIII, 1872, pp309-310. This supposed beacon at 'Greiston' should not be confused with the **beacon at Tankerton** (now represented by a replica), which was part of the national warning system; nor with the **local mariners' beacons** maintained by fishermen.
White HT, '**The Beacon System in Kent**', AC v. XLVI, 1934, pp.77-96.
25. Collard AO, '**The Oyster and Dredgers of Whitstable**', Joseph Collard London 1902 p.59. (reference: building remains).
Cox WJ, 'Illustrated Popular **Guide to Whitstable-on-Sea**', Whitstable n/d p.48. (reference: 'Grayes').
26. Goodsall RH, ref 16. above, p.147.
27. Wallenberg JK ref 7. above, v. 1 p.278.
28. WT 6.6.1953.
29. Abstract, ref 1 above, pp.1-3 (given as Patent Roll 1483, 22/23 Edward IV Pt 11. M23; exemplification of Plea de Quo Warranto, 6 Ed II). For fuller history see ref. 40 below pp.34-35.
30. The **Borough of Harwich** (see map page 45) - identifying the precise boundaries of the Borough seems to be impossible. Originally these were marked, at least in part, by mark stones, called 'Donkey Stones' locally, but these have all disappeared. A map of c. 1770 drawn up for Seasalter in a dispute over the boundary of the oyster fisheries (Whitstable Museum Wallace Harvey archive, and Kent Archive Office TR781/2) shows very clearly Area (1) north of the Canterbury Road, but not its extension on the south side. Area

(2) is very exactly drawn and shows how curiously the parish boundary did not fit that of the Borough. For area (3) only its western end is indicated.
For Area (3) the only source seems to be the boundary as marked on the OS 25" sheet of 1872; this however has distinct differences from 1770 in the other two areas.

31. Keith-Lucas B, ref 11. above p.153. The adjacent part of the 'Whitstable' area was divided into three 'boroughs': Bullen, Bourn, and Grimgill.
32. Wallenberg JK, ref 7. above, v 2, p217.
    Ward G, '**The Origins of Whitstable**', AC v LVII pp.51-55. Suggests that the 'white pillar or post' was most likely a boundary mark at the junction of the parishes of Whitstable, Seasalter and Harwich, somewhere in the area of today's High street. This could then have become a meeting point, leading to a market, and a town developing. Thus Ward proposes that there was a settlement in this situation in 1086; though not recorded in Domesday. A view which is not accepted here.
    Baldwin R, '**Seasalter: A Problem Borough in Domesday** Kent Re-examined. AC v. CX 1992, p.237. A very complex argument which concludes with the suggestion that it was the place recorded in Domesday book as 'Seasalter' which was actually situated in the area known as the borough of Harwich. Again proposing that the settlement which ultimately became Whitstable town had its origin in Saxon times.
    There is however no direct documentary or any archaeological evidence, so far, to support this thesis. As discussed in this book, the tiny fishing village shown on the map of 1725 (now represented by the wider west end of Harbour Street) was called 'Harwich'. It probably dates no earlier as a village settlement than the sixteenth century.
33. It is interesting to note that in 1693 the Best family of Canterbury sold the land lying on the east side of the little village: this was the ancient field earlier called 'Hammells' and at this time '**Old House Field**' (the 'old house; being the isolated building east of letter 'L' on the 1725 map). This sale then stimulated the growth of the street eastward.
    It would appear that the community was prospering and expanding by the later seventeenth century, leading to building development.
34. **Dickens C, Ed 'the Happy Fishing Grounds**' in 'All the Year Round', 26.11.1859, written by journalist J Hollingshead.
35. Descent of the Manor of Whitstable, see ref. 16 above
36. Goodsall RH, ref. 16 above, p.19.
37. Abstract ref. 1 above, p.9.
38. Hussey A, '**Testamenta Cantiana**. A series of extracts from fifteenth and sixteenth century wills relating to church building and topography', London 1907, p.362.
39. The **manor was sold** to Edward Foad and James Smith 11/12th October, 1791. James Smith then resold so that the land portion (the Salts) became the property of Nutt, Salisbury and Foad; the Oyster Fishery was purchased by Thomas Foord who held it until the Freemen could become owners under Act of Parliament, 1793. The title and the Tankerton land was a separate purchase by Charles Pearson in 1794.
    Copies of the complex legal documents for these transactions are to be found in a) the deeds for the Castle and the Harbour held by Canterbury City Council, b) in the records of the Whitstable Oyster Company.
40. Pike G, Cann J, Lambert R, '**Oysters and Dredgermen**', Compass Publications Whitstable 1992.

5 BARN HOUSE - AN ANCIENT MANOR RESTORED

On that Friday evening when the young Miss Dot Carson was asked to take her car to meet the mid-day train next day she thought little of it. Being a member of the Voluntary Aid Detachment she assumed that some wounded soldiers needed transporting to one of the hospitals along at Tankerton. Saturday 15th September 1915 turned out, however, to be a memorable experience for her and a 'red letter day' for the town. Her passenger she was told early in the morning would be none other than Queen Mary. 'I was terrified,' she recalled later, 'I nearly had a fit when I heard I was to drive the Queen.'[1]

The Daimler was brought out and hurriedly polished. Then a problem arose: slightly built Dot Carson found swinging the starting handle a great difficulty; what an embarrassment might arise at the station. To the rescue came neighbour Frank Tyars, who lent his coachman, the aptly named Mr

Queen Mary arrives by car at Barn House

Speed, to follow the car on his bicycle and apply the required muscle power for the return journey. At five minutes past twelve o'clock the train steamed into Whitstable station with the Royal Pullman coach attached. Out stepped Her Majesty accompanied by one lady-in-waiting only, for this was a private visit. Indeed there was only a handful of spectators to raise a cheer outside. For security reasons the visit had been kept a secret. So Dot Carson drove away, 'a competent driver', she replied to the Queen's gentle enquiry. It was, in fact, the first time that Her Majesty had been driven by a woman.

Their destination was Barn House in Joy Lane: a large part-timbered Tudor-style residence, then on the fringe of the town. Three years earlier on July 6th, 1912, 'Queen Mary's Holiday Home for Working Girls' had been opened there[2]. It was established with the sum of £12,500 contributed as a Coronation Gift to the new Queen by the 'Mary's of the Empire'. The Home was run in collaboration with the London Girls' Club Union and its purpose was to provide a short break of some two or three weeks for 'those who most require rest and freedom from worry'. They would doubtless be the better class of working girl from shops and offices, though even they might work a ten hour day.

The Holiday Home provided accommodation for 14 girls at a time. There were four bedrooms: three sleeping four girls and the fourth two. Each bed was covered with a quilt worked by the Whitstable Ladies' Knitting Guild embroidered with the letters QMH surmounted by a crown[3]. The girls were required to keep their rooms clean and tidy, otherwise they might read, play indoor games, enjoy tennis or croquet on the lawn, or visit the shelter on the beach.

Queen Mary had taken a close interest in this project, sending tapestries and furniture from the royal palaces. The royal patronage was emphasised by numerous portraits on the walls.

Why had Whitstable been so honoured? As described in Chapter Ten, from the 1890s the town had attracted a number of notable residents, some temporary and some permanent, who sought to escape from the noise, grime and bustle of the capital for the quietness and fresh air of this little town, and yet be within easy reach of London by rail. Whitstable was rural but not remote. It was a Mrs Sydney Leo with contacts in the court circle who recommended this area to those administering the 'Home' project on behalf of the Queen. She had spent some six months at Whitstable for the recuperation of her husband after a serious illness. Mrs Leo was herself recommended the fresh sea air by her friend Mrs HB Irving who, as we shall see, had fallen in love with the windmill on Borstal Hill and its splendid views out across the bay.

Queen Mary met each of the fourteen girls in residence and then proceeded to tour the building, displaying the curiosity that was a life-long characteristic. Greta Dawson, whose father George Reeves had owned the house, recalls:

'Miss Campbell was matron of the Home and she had two dogs, Zeth and Curly, which she adored. But she did not want them to be a nuisance to the Queen, so she had them shut up in her cottage at the end of the garden, facing Alexandra Road.

'When Miss Campbell was accompanying the queen on a tour round the grounds, there on the lawn was - a bone. Nothing escaped Her Majesty. "I see you have dogs, Miss Campbell!' she said. The matron explained the situation, and then Queen Mary insisted that Zeth and Curly should be let out and soon made friends with them.

'Lots of us remember Kate, who was cook at Barn House in those days. Kate was a dear, but on the untidy side. When she knew the Queen was coming she pushed everything she could lay her hands on into the cupboard under the stairs, and kept her fingers crossed that Her Majesty would not want to look inside.

'As usual, interested in everything, the Queen pointed at the cupoard door and asked where it led. Poor Kate had to say, "That's my bogey-hole, mam!" and opened up to show the jumble inside. Her Majesty smiled and said, "a very satisfactory bogey-hole, I'm sure."'[4]

After a light lunch the Queen was driven down to the girls' bathing cabin on West Beach, passing through 'Irish Village' which she found 'most picturesque'.

Before her departure, Queen Mary gave to the matron a parcel of men's pyjamas and slippers, for her visit had been precipitated by the decision to replace the girls with wounded soldiers from October 1st. The visit ended with the return journey to the station through streets now crowded with townsfolk: women and children cheered and men doffed caps and hats as the car passed by.

So concluded the only royal visit to Whitstable. The local newspaper saluted the occasion with the banner headline 'An Historic Event for the World's Famous Oyster Town'. As a memento of her role on that day Dot Carson received a letter of thanks on behalf of Queen Mary, and, as a personal gesture, a signed photograph of Her Majesty: a much treasured possession throughout her life[5].

It is not recorded if the Queen expressed an interest in Barn House itself as she toured the building. In later life she showed a great enthusiasm for things antique; was she perhaps intrigued with this curious blend of something old and yet not quite genuine?

Back in 1906 this site had been occupied by an old building divided into two cottages and joining on to a thatched barn[6]. The property was attached to Little Joy Farm nearby. George Reeves, a well known builder,

decided to buy the buildings, demolish them, and salvage materials for the mock Tudor houses which it was his passion to build.

But for one of those strokes of good fortune which dot the stories of local history Barn House might never have come into being, and an intriguing remnant of earlier history swept away. By chance George Reeves decided to show his purchase to an architect acquaintance Oswald Wylson. Entering the barn section Mr Wylson looked up at the roof timbers and immediately identified the central feature as a splendid crown post. On closer examination he suggested that this would have been part of the structure of an open hall, a building probably of the fifteenth century, and forming part of a medieval manor house[7].

Under the feudal system all land and authority was vested in the Crown. Grants were made by the King in return for allegiance, representing the King's authority, and providing military support when necessary. Land was therefore held in 'lordship' and individual holdings were termed 'manors'. These might vary in size from a single village to great blocks of country forming a large estate. One of the great Barons might hold perhaps a hundred or more manors scattered across the country. Many of these would be granted to lesser nobility, the knights, who in turn pledged allegiance and service to their overlord: hence a manor was said to be held by 'knight's service'. The peasantry on the individual manor held their land-holding by acknowledging the authority of their lord and rendering him certain services. Feudal society was therefore pyramid-shaped and composed of layers, each of which owed allegiance and gave services to the layer above, until the king was reached at the apex. For practical reasons many services gradually became 'commuted' into monetary payments.

As we have seen in the previous chapter, the King might also grant, not land, but some aspect of his rights and authority. These were valued because they carried with them the right to receive payments or to raise taxes. Thus the Manor of Whitstable implied rights, including overseeing justice, over an administrative district, the 'Hundred'.

From details recorded by Hasted in his 'History of Kent' the site of Barn House can be identified with the manor of Cundies Hall or Place[8]. The name is first recorded in the holder of the manor in the reign of Edward I (late thirteenth century), John de Cundishall, who held it by knight's service of Walter de Clifford, a leading baron of the time. A descendant of his with the same name, a man of 'high character for his courage', defeated one of King

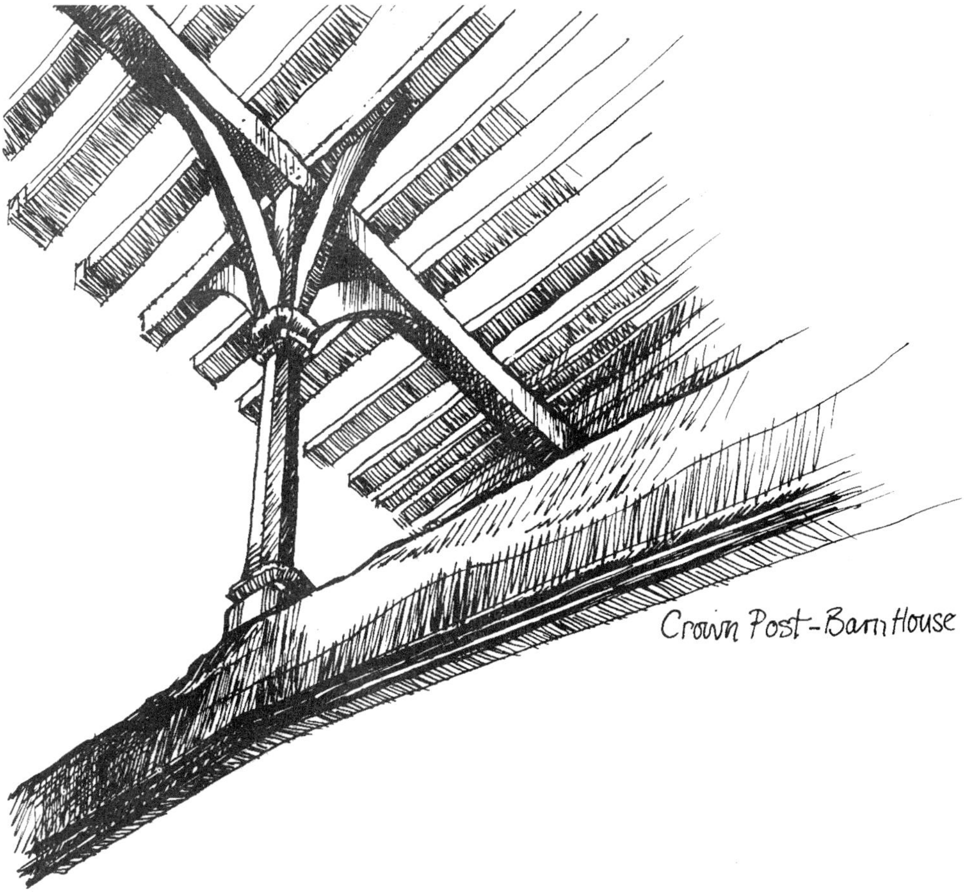

Edward III's enemies in single combat and took him prisoner. For this he was rewarded with £30 'out of the king's staple at Canterbury' (that was the tax paid on cloth). The manor later passed into the Roper family, great landowners in this area 'whose estates in this parish it became afterwards so blended that it entirely lost all memory of its former name.' The Roper family had a great mansion in St Dunstan's at Canterbury of which only the Tudor gateway remains today almost opposite the church.

This map of the hamlet of 'Bostall', as Borstal was then called, dated 1730, shows quite a large house in the position of the old manor, so it would seem the decline in the two cottages occurred later than this.

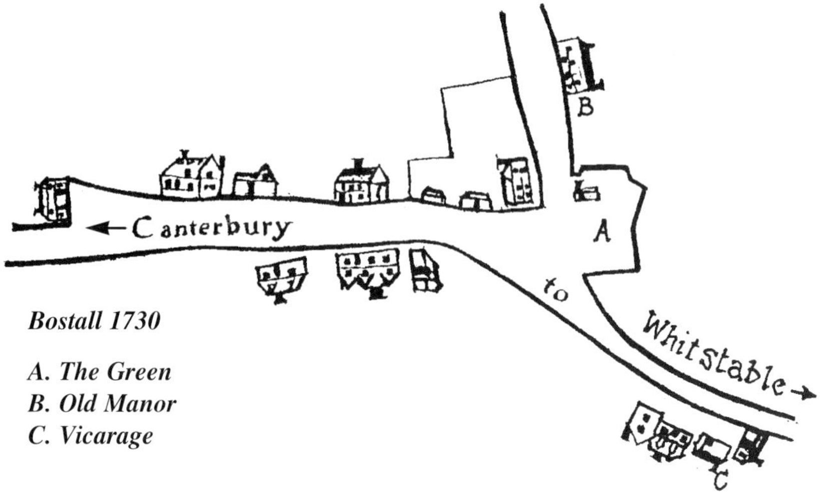

Bostall 1730

A. The Green
B. Old Manor
C. Vicarage

The open space shown on the map at the junction of the two roads must be 'Bostall Green'. It was here about seven o'clock in the evening of the 5th July 1736 that the local men were 'playing crickett' as a later court record described. Suddenly quarrelling broke out between two of the spectators, Martha Wood and Walter Webster. 'Several High Words Past between them' during which Webster called Martha 'an Impudent Whore'. Around were her mother and neighbours, and one of these, William Hobday a blacksmith, gave evidence on what had occurred when Martha brought a charge of defamation against Webster[9]. He stated that all present understood that Martha had been accused of the 'the crime of Fornication or Inconstancy', although as far as he knew she was 'a Person of Virtuous Character'. This court case records a very early example of village cricket as well as recreating a glimpse of the life in the community depicted on the map of 'Bostall Green'.

Local place names and topography are often the keys to unlocking the fundamental history of an area. The name 'Bostall' (now Borstal), for example, derives from the Old English 'borgsteall' meaning a protected or defended place. This suggests its origin as a newly established settlement in wild countryside, probably in the late Saxon period. Early documents help to illustrate this process of settlement. In Saxon charters land holdings in a very wide area are intitially described just as being 'bi northanwude' - to the north of the wood - that is the great belt of the Forest of Blean[10]. But by 1086 in the Domesday survey only the Archbishop's holding here is described as 'Nortone", north-wood. Seasalter (Sesaltre) and Swalecliffe (Soancliffe) are now separately identified[11]. So by this time a manorial pattern of settlement had become established. The process of 'taming' these lands 'north of the wood' was initially carried out by the great monastic institutions who established tiny churches to act as focal points in these thinly populated lands[12]. Although, as discussed in Chapter Three on the Graveney boat, at Seasalter there was a place of early development.

This spread of occupation north of the Blean can be closely related to the topography of the local area as shown in the diagram. There are three basic divisions. First the very flat low-lying coastal lands, originally marshland and formerly extending much further seaward. From this the higher ground rises, either directly along the coast in low cliffs, or further inland in slopes, often very steep and scarp-like as at Borstal Hill. This higher ground often has broad, almost plateau-like areas as at Tankerton and Chestfield. On the southern side the ground falls, again in places with steep slopes as along Clapham Hill, to a broad trough-like valley. The third division of the landscape is marked by steep slopes rising up to the plateau of the Blean Forest. In brief, we have the coastal marshland, the undulating open country, and the woodland and heath of the Blean.

Archaeological evidence suggests that the broad band of 'open country' was never heavily wooded and was cleared and cultivated to some extent from later prehistoric times, though no major settlement sites have yet been found[13]. By the early middle ages this land was being farmed under the manorial system with a number of large manor houses and related smaller farms. As mentioned earlier there was Cundies Hall at Borstal, and nearby

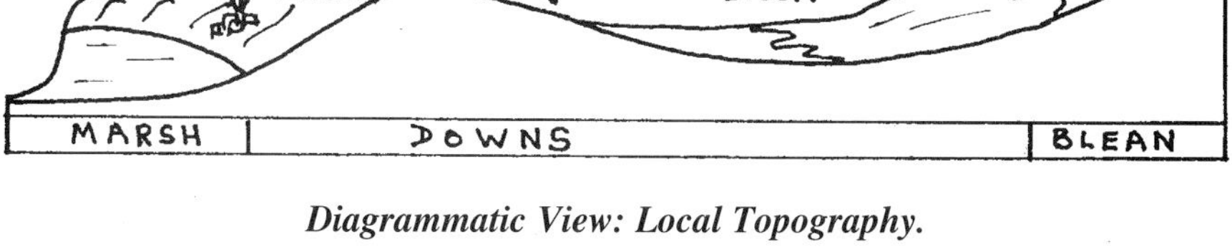

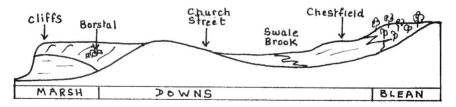

Diagrammatic View: Local Topography.

Grimshill Manor; at Tankerton there was St Anne's, and probably at Church Street a 'lost' manor called in early documents 'Northwood', a last survivor of this ancient designation. Further east was the large farm at Rayham, and then beyond the Swale Brook the Court Lodge by Swalecliffe Church and the manor at Chestfield. Many parts of this open farmland were described as 'down' land: Martin-down, Duncan Down, Cuckoo Down and May-down: these names record owners of the land probably in the sixteenth century. Until the present century this entire area had only a small and scattered population. In a few places hamlets grew up as at Borstal, Seasalter, Church Street and Swalecliffe, but these were no more than groups of farms and cottages stretched along the roads, as at Borstal.

Just as the coastal marshes had an important economic value in their fish, oyster grounds, salt production and summer grazing, so the Blean was exploited in the local economy. Recent archaeological investigation suggests that in this now wooded country there was some cultivation in the later prehistoric and Roman periods[14]. Probably the change to a wetter and colder climate caused it to revert to scrubland (as the name 'blean' implies) from the fifth century AD. In the medieval period the cover of heath, bush and oak trees provided valuable 'pannage' for pigs and 'herbage' for cattle. The droveways by which the animals were moved to and fro often survive today as trackways and footpaths, giving a north-south grain to the landscape. In places clearings were made in the edge of the Blean and this is recorded in names such as Ellenden, Thornden and Clowes - 'den' and 'cluse' both mean clearing. Points of entry into the Blean are indicated by names with 'gate' endings: Radfall Gate, Broomfield Gate and Bleangate[15]. In the later middle ages the Blean was developed as woodland, giving it the character it has today with large sections still exploited as coppice.

Much of the landscape north of the remaining Blean today is covered by the urban sprawl of Whitstable which has now submerged the old settlements of Seasalter and Swalecliffe. The visitor might be forgiven, then, for feeling that there is little of the past obviously remaining. Chestfield, however, would seem to have the character of a traditional old village with its numerous half-timbered houses and the picturesque group of ancient barn, oast houses and the brick and timber golf-club house at the centre. Yet one might perhaps look around in vain for the village church.

It is surprising then to realise that until well into the present century Chestfield as a community did not exist; this remained a landscape of open farmland unchanged in essence since the middle ages. The name Chestfield derives from the Saxon 'caet haerst' meaning wooded 'forest', where as a charter of AD946 records, the men of Swalecliffe had the right to cut timber[16]. With the first word actually pronounced 'chat' this name had become by the thirteenth century 'Chethurst' and then rendered in Norman French as 'Chestville'. A fourteenth century taxation list records the manorial organisation: a central manor held by James de Chestville, and then the surrounding farms of Balsar Street, Highgate, and Bodkin[17]. This situation continued, with little change except for the creation of several other farms, down to the twentieth century. When the Manor Estate was sold in 1920 it still comprised 700 acres of farmland covering most of the Chestfield area.

Now an amazing change was to take place for the purchaser was none other than Mr George Reeves, the creator of Barn House[18].

On the basis of his experience and the profit from his building work which included a number of pseudo-Tudor houses, Mr Reeves was set to realise his lifetime's ambition: the planning and building of an 'old world' village of part-timbered houses, with himself playing the role of Lord of the Manor. Initially he lived in the manor house and there planned the layout of his 'model' village. Nearby was the great tithe barn which he divided and used as the basis of two elaborate mock-Tudor houses. These look particularly authentic, for the timber and stone materials came from the destruction of Hales Place at Hackington, and much of this dated from the reign of Queen Elizabeth I. Indeed, it had in its turn incorporated stonework obtained from the destruction of St Augustine's Abbey at Canterbury. There is no doubt that the large rose window in 'The Paddock' and much of the other stonework had an ecclesiastical origin (illustrations pp. 66-67).

The few old cottages were incorporated in larger houses, and to form the centre-piece of his village George Reeves used the buildings at Balsar Street farm. The great thatched barn, said to date back to the fourteenth century, was restored, and the old building of three cottages, originally the farmhouse, was converted into the clubhouse for his golf course. These old buildings, together with the late nineteenth century oast houses, do indeed form a very attractive group.

The estate was laid out on a generous scale with the substantial timbered houses in large plots, and the smaller cottage-style houses grouped around greens. One of the old drove ways was incorporated into the estate plan as 'The Drove'; it continues towards the woods as a footpath across the golf

course. Highgate Farm was demolished but the significance of its name - the upper way - was recalled in the name of the road, 'The Ridgeway'.

In his grand style George Reeves planned a polo ground (remembered in Polo Way), and provided, in addition to the golf course, a cricket ground, tennis courts and a bowling green. There was a dairy, and produce from the allotments and orchards was sold at his shop near 'The Barn'. He envisaged Chestfield village as being as self-sufficient as possible. Besides being the property developer, Mr Reeves ran virtually every aspect of the community: in figure, manner and style he was 'Lord of the Manor'. But in 1941 financial problems caused him to sell the estate and this saw the end of his style of building; from then on Chestfield developed in a more conventional manner.

George Reeves not only realised his ideal at Chestfield, he also gave to the Whitstable area generally a feeling that part-timbered buildings were indigenous to this part of Kent. He was particularly successful through his use of old materials: the destruction of genuine old houses elsewhere enabled him to create a sense of authenticity. It is a tribute to his vision that the central part of Chestfield has now been designated a Conservation Area, to preserve the special character of his village.

Barn House, however, was the most interesting of George Reeves' reconstructions because it incorporated some original medieval timber work and preserved in his special blend of the authentic and the imitation a place of genuine antiquity. It was a true 'manor house' to which Queen Mary came.

References

1. WT 25.9.1915. **Queen Mary's visit.**
2. WT 11.11.1911: Purchase and **restoration of Barn House.**
3. WT 6.7.1912. The 'Home' described.
4. Woodman G and G, '**We Remember Whitstable**', Pryor Publications Whitstable 2nd Ed 1988, p.72.
5. WT 3.6.77. Account of the Queen's visit with photographs.
6. The original cottages are distantly seen in a photograph taken down Borstal Hill: Whitstable Museum Wallace Harvey collection.
7. WT ref. 2 above.
8. **Hasted** E, 'The History and topographical survey of the County of Kent', 2nd Ed. in 12 vols. 1797-1801, Edition EP Publishing Co Ltd 1972, v. VIII, p. 512 v. VIII p.512
9. Deposition by William Hobday, records of the Court of St Augustine, Canterbury Cathedral Archive PRC 18/51.

'Map of a Farm at **Borstal-Green** in the Parish of Seasalter in the County of Kent belonging to Capt Richard Clement 1730', in deeds of the Jolly Sailor public house, Muniment Room, Fremlin Brewery Maidstone.

10. Ward G, 'The **Origins of Whitstable**', AC v. LVII 1944, p.51.
    Wallenberg JK, 'The **Place Names of Kent**', Upsalla 1934, v. 2 p.493
11. Morgan P, Ed. 'The **Domesday Book of Kent**', Phillimore Chichester 1983: Whitstable 2.14; Seasalter 3.10; Swalecliffe 5.139.
    The Domesday Book entry for Whitstable (Nortone) is discussed in Chapter 4.
12. Drewett P, Ruddling D, Gardiner M, '**The South East to AD1000**', Longman 1988, pp.316-17.
13. Canterbury **Archaeological Trust: Survey** for the Thanet Way Public Inquiry, Kent County Council 1992, Whitstable Museuem archive.

14. Wheaton A, **Blean Woods** Archaeological Research Group, report Spring 1989 p.9. Canterbury City Library, Local Studies collection.
15. Trust survey, ref. 13 above, pp.3-4
16. Whitlock D, '**English Historical Documents c.500-1042**', London 1955, p.341.
17. Chestfield Parish Council Magazine, Nov 1991: Perkins D, '**Chestfield Manor Estate**'.
18. WT 12.7.1941, obituary of **George Reeves**.

'The Paddocks" constructed. from the Tithe Barn.

6 THE ROLE OF THE TURNPIKE ROAD

Descending the main road down Borstal Hill there suddenly comes into view the splendid panorama of Whitstable bay with the buildings of the town crowded up to the shore. The scene is most striking on a sunny Sunday with a morning tide when many yachts dot the sparkling blue sea, giving some reminder of former days when these waters were full of ships of sail. At the bottom of the hill, the road bends towards the main part of the town and here a curious small building stands, as though dumped in the middle of the roadway. This can be recognised as a toll-house, one of the many survivors of the Turnpike Roads which were once a vital part of the country's comunication network. Here, though, it is perhaps surprising to see one at the entrance to what must have been quite a small town.

The great expanse of the bay and the little toll-house - the link between these two underlies the early development of the town of Whitstable. The

The view of Whitstable from the top of Borstal Hill.

waters of the bay gave shelter to ships and their cargoes, and the roadway provided the link between the coast and the city of Canterbury. By the eighteenth century Whitstable had become the main port for the city.

For Roman Canterbury, 'Durovernum', the main commercial artery was the River Stour. This continued for centuries for goods were more easily moved by water than by land. By the sixteenth century changes to the coastline of East Kent had severely restricted access to the Stour, and severe silting of the river bed limited its navigation[1]. As a result, while Fordwich continued as a port, river transport beyond, even for barges, was limited or even impossible. Goods therefore had be moved at greater expense overland.

By the reign of Henry VIII Canterbury's concern was expressed in an Act of Parliament in 1515. This had the intention 'to make that part of the

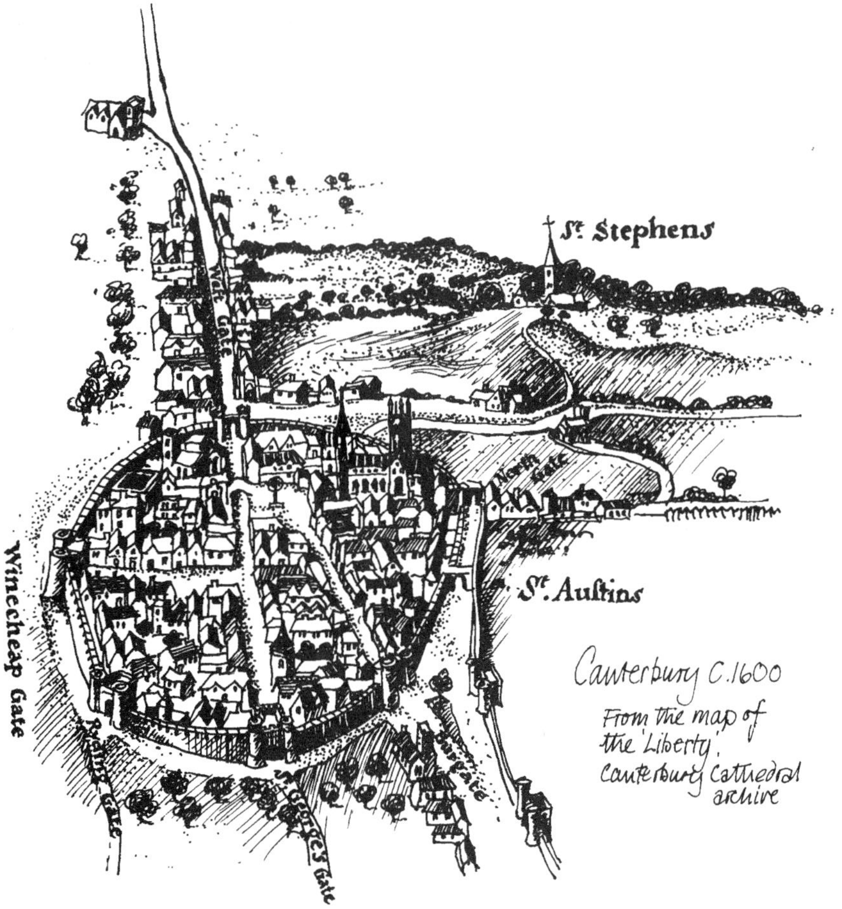

Canterbury C.1600
From the map of the 'Liberty', Canterbury Cathedral archive

river between Fordwich and Canterbury answerable to that below the former; that is to cleanse, deepen and enlarge it...'[2]. It seems that nothing came from this and so in 1588 the city corporation took action: 'A large Sum is laid out in scouring the River Stour, and a level is taken, with a view to making it navigable. The money is raised on the inhabitants by an assessment'[3]. In 1591 the City Record notes that 'Lighters go between Canterbury and Fordwich'. However what improvement there was seems not to have lasted and across the seventeenth century further attempts were made, this time by individuals venturing their capital in return for a proportion of the landing dues. These enterprises also failed to make any significant improvement.

Daniel Defoe on his great tour through England and Wales in the early

1720s summed up the contemporary situation. The City, he wrote: 'are obliged to fetch all their heavy goods, either from Fordwich, three miles off, or from Whitstable seven miles off; the latter they chuse for such heavy goods as come from London; as oyl, wine, grocery, etc., because 'tis the less hazard by sea, but as for coals, deals, etc., they come by way of Sandwich, and are brought up the river to Fordwich'[4].

So what must have been originally a collection of fishermen's cottages along the Whitstable shore was now becoming established as an organised port for Canterbury. Significant landings here perhaps date back to the settled conditions of Tudor times and the rapid growth then of both coastal and continental trading: in 1537 the 'hoye' of John See is recorded at Whitstable[5].

The detailed Customs records surviving for the later seventeenth century show two fleets of vessels operating in these waters, thirteen mainly carrying coal from Sunderland and fifteen being involved with London. From London came domestic goods as illustrated by the manifest for a vessel, 15th April 1692[6]:

1/2 barrels soap	*3 rundletts ayle*
7 pigs of ore fodder	*3 bags bottom cotton*
Lead eight bags shott	*3 rundletts ayle one like vinegar*
1 cwt. Woollen drapery and mercury	*1 paper parcell 4 boxes apothecary wares*
1 cwt. parcell linen drapery	*1 bundle one parcell-and pork*
1 pipe canary 4 hampers bottle wine	*3 one barrel tarr*
1 of brandy	*1 bag 2 doz brooms and cork*
5 cwt. cheese	*1 chest oranges and lemons*
2 baskets 5 boxes felt caster hatts cases	*1 matt glue and 1 doz.blacking*
2 doz. boxes 2 parcells haberdashery	*1 basket 1 box earthenware glasses*
6 ton grocery	

Return cargoes to the capital usually included wheat, oats, hops and malt, and quantities of Canterbury worsted. From time to time some tons of copperas are listed; it would also have been to the copperas quays that some of the 'chaldrons' of coal came. The role this landing point played in the larger trade with Canterbury as against the Horsebridge boat road at Whitstable is not known. (Copperas works, map of 1770 p. 42).

The local customs records made under the Port of Faversham show that the volume of trade at Whitstable was relatively small. For the last decade of the seventeenth century of 298 shipments listed only 40 were for

Whitstable; there being 44 along the coast at Herne and the remainder at Faversham itself[7].

As trade gradually increased so did the traffic by pack horses and lumbering waggons between the coast and Canterbury. We saw in Chapter Two that there may well have been an established route in Roman times from the city, passing through Blean to Pean Hill before turning down to the coast at Seasalter (map p. 15). This could then have easily been extended as a trackway through Borstal down to the sea-shore by Whitstable. Records suggest that this path had been trodden for centuries, for as early as 1312 Whitstable's Lord of the Manor was claiming as an established privilege a market stall for his fishermen tenants in the High Street of Canterbury, as we have seen in Chapter Four. And John Roper, one of the great landowners whose mansion lay just outside the West Gate, left in 1523 the large sum of 100 marks for the benefit of the citizens: 'to the making of an horse way for the fisshe wyves and other, in the highway from Whitstaple to the entring of the strete of saincte Dunston'[8].

By the early eighteenth century this route had become so important to

The original Turnpike and Tollgate 1850

Canterbury that a Turnpike was established by Act of Parliament. The tolls would pay for improvements beyond the repairs which were the duty of the Parishes through which it passed. The preamble to the Bill stated:

'the road from Saint Dunstan's Cross near the City of Canterbury... to the waterside at Whitstable... is in many parts thereof very narrow and the said road, by reason of many heavy Carriages and a great number of Passsengers passing through the same, is in the Winter Season become ruinous and unsafe for Travellers and Carriages, notwithstanding the inhabitants of the several Parishes through which the said Road leads, have constantly every year performed their respective Works required by the Laws now in being, towards repairing the same; Wherefore, and to the Intent that the Road aforesaid from Saint Dunstan's Cross, near Canterbury, to the Waterside at Whitstable aforesaid, may, with all convenient speed, be effectually amended and enlarged...'[9]

The first road turnpiked in Kent was from Sevenoaks through to Tunbridge Wells in 1710 and this was followed in stages by Watling Street as far as Canterbury. So the inclusion of the road to Whitstable in 1736 illustrates its importance to Canterbury both for the transport of goods, especially coal for developing industries, and for passenger traffic using hoys as a means of travelling to and from the capital. In that year this advertisement appeared in the Kentish Post:

Richard Read, Master of the Richard and Elizabeth Hoy, will set Sail (God willing) from Whitstable to London every Saturday; and carries all sorts of Goods, and Passengers. He is to be spoke with... at the Sign of the Castle... Canterbury, every Friday and Saturday, where Goods will be taken in.'[10]

The act itemised a variety of conveyances: 'Coach, Berlin, Chariot, Calash, Chaise, Hearse, or Litter' with charges ranging from one shilling for four or more horses, down to three pence for one horse. And similarly for a 'Waggon, Wain, Cart, or other such Carriage' the charge went from eight pence for three horses to three pence for one. Then 'for every Horse, Mare, Gelding, Mule, Ass, laden or unladen, and not drawing, the Sum of One Penny.' For livestock the rate was ten pence per score for oxen, cows, or 'neat cattle', and for the calves, hogs and lambs, five pence. The penalty for avoiding a toll was not to exceed forty shillings, one half going to the informant and the other to the Trustees.

Exemptions were many, recognising the needs of local farmers, those on official business and journeys warranting compassion. So the transport of materials for repairing the road, and the movement of crops, materials and implements as well as livestock between fields and farm was toll free. So, too, were persons attending religious worship or a funeral (but not apparently a wedding), then exempted also were clergy about their parochial duties, the carriage of postal mail, soldiers on duty, patients bound for hospital and vagrants being expelled from a parish. One might also travel without payment journeying to and from an election.

The reaction of local people to the restriction on their movements is not recorded, but it is likely, as elsewhere, that toll collectors were sometimes intimidated, tolls not paid, and country by-ways used to circumvent the system. One important repercussion lay in the Trustees' right to take beach material for repairs to the road; the enormous quantities recorded must have lessened the natural defences of the coast line and in places accelerated erosion.

In 1860 the main line railway from London arrived at Whitstable, as described in the next chapter. Involved was the building of a bridge across the main road into the town only a few yards from the Turnpike. Perhaps to facilitate construction and certainly in recognition of the growth of Whitstable beyond this point, the tollgate and the keeper's cottage were moved to the bottom of Borstal Hill. Here the Turnpike continued to operate until closure under national legislation on 1st November 1871.

There the toll-keeper's cottage remains, a reminder of a major period in our transport history. It survives into a time when the introduction of toll-roads is again under discussion; as so often history turns full circle.

References

1. Wyman J, '**The Decay of Fordwich as a Port**' in McIntosh KM, Ed. 'Fordwich... the lost port', Ramsgate 1975, p.201.
2. **Hasted** E, 'The History and topographical survey of the County of Kent', 2nd Ed. in 12 vols. 1797-1801, Edition EP Publishing Co Ltd 1972, v XII p.139.
3. Hasted E, 'Minutes... from the ancient Records', appendix, v xii, pp.640-1.
4. **Defoe** D, 'A **Tour through England and Wales** Divided into Circuits of Journies', 1724-26, Ed. Everyman Dent 1962, v.1 p.119.
5. Burwash D, '**English Merchant Shipping, 1460-1540**', David and Charles 1969 p.132.
6. Harvey W, '**The Merchant Ships of Whitstable**', Emprint Whitstable 1993, p.15.
7. Andrews J, 'The **Trade of the Port of Faversham 1650-1750**' AC v. LXIX 1955, p.128.
8. Goodsall R, '**Whitstable, Seasalter and Swalecliffe. The History** of Three Kent Parishes', Canterbury 1938, pp.26-27.
9. **Turnpike Bill** (9.Geo.11, C.10.), Canterbury Local Studies Collection, ref. 222055. Keith-Lucas B, 'Parish Affairs', Kent County Council Library, Chap 6 'The **Turnpikes**' p.83.
10. Kentish Post and Newsletter, 7.9.1726.

The return of Trooper Butcher from the Boer War

7 RAILWAY STATION AND BRIDGE

It was a dull day in Whitstable, Thursday 20th December 1900: the sky was heavy with cloud and rain threatened on a strengthening keen wind. But no matter, for if the weather was dreary the town was not - Whitstable was, in the newspaper's favourite expression, 'en fete'. There was a feeling of excitement in the air: along the main street flags and bunting flapped in the breeze; patriotic mottoes abounded on the buildings. 'Whitstable put forth every effort available, and the eclat which characterised the whole was most refreshing.'[1]

As midday approached crowds thronged the main thoroughfare and all was bustle and excitement in the vicinity of the station. Here were drawn up detachments from the Army, the Navy and the Coastguard. Above, on the crowded platform, were assembled senior citizens of the town headed by the Chairman of the recently appointed first Town Council.

At a few minutes past twelve o'clock the train drew in, and from a carriage stepped 'the hero of the hour'. Handsome in his Yeomanry uniform with its dashing hat turned up at one side, Trooper Butcher was home from the war in distant South Africa: that campaign to teach the Boers a lesson. To hearty cheers he was welcomed by the Chairman of the Council and congratulated upon his safe return. He greeted his family and then descended

the stairs to the street where he was met with tremendous cheering from the assembled throng.

Trooper Butcher then entered the carriage drawn by a pair of horses which formed the centre of the great procession. First came a mounted detachment of Yeomanry, the Town Band, a Royal Navy detachment, then men from the Free Foresters, the Hand and Heart Society, the Oddfellows, followed by the Fire Brigade and the boys from the Trust and Board Schools 'looking particularly smart with their sashes and bows of patriotic colours' with their Headmasters and Assistants. Then followed Representatives of the Parish Council, the School Board and the Urban District Council, the Drum and Fife Band, followed by the Coastguards and the dismounted Yeomanry. Then came the hero of the day accompanied by father, uncles and the Council Chairman. Behind marched a group of his comrades in arms; the Order of Buffaloes to which he belonged; then the Charity Trustees; the Gas and Water Company Directors, and, bringing up the rear, the military band. Here were the men of Whitstable on parade!

Slowly this great company moved through the town, cheered along its way to the Jubilee Fountain at Tankerton Parade. Here an Illuminated Address was presented:

In the name of your native town of Whitstable, we welcome you home from your year's campaign in South Africa, where you have taken a soldier's part in one of the greatest of our British wars. For your safety in sickness and on many battlefields we thank God, and congratulate you... You were one of the foremost in the band of Kentish heroes to set the example of Imperial patriotism and cross the ocean to fight alongside with our Colonial Volunteers for that flag which never waves but over free peoples... So long as her sons, carrying their lives in their hands come forward to offer themselves in her service in the hour of need... so long will our dear Fatherland hold up its head among unfriendly nations as being under God's guidance, one of His chief civilising instruments throughout the world.'

The procession returned to St Alphege Church for a thanksgiving service, naturally opening with 'Onward Christian Soldiers' and then to a luncheon at the Duke of Cumberland for the reception committee and Trooper Butcher with the whole of the Yeomanry contingent.

'Apart from the fact that the Hero received a watch from officialdom and that many toasts were drunk, we know no more than can be heard through the Cumberland's closed doors.

'Licensing laws were elastic then and there is no doubt the reception continued until gaslights went out and candles climbed the stairs to bed.

'Whitstable was satisfied. It had feted its Hero and never had there been such a day'.[2]

Alas - when the euphoria of the day had died down a terrible truth slowly dawned upon the population:

The Hero, intentionally or not, was not as enthusiasm had made him.

'Generals Buller and White had got on all right without him, Baden

Powell had out-skirmished the Boer commandos alone, and Ladysmith and Mafeking been relieved without his help. Kopje and veldt had never echoed, rock hard, to his army boots or the hooves of his horse.

'All he had done was to stay in Table Bay looking after horses and never been within a hundred miles of the fighting.

'The only time in recorded history when Whitstable had gone wild was over an illusion. It was the fans who had been taken for a ride, not the hero.'

The town lapsed into embarrassed silence on the matter. At root the jingoism of the time, the desire to rival Canterbury's welcome to returning veterans, and the ambition of the town's first Council to lead the way - all these together accounted for this explosion of local pride. Sadly, when real heroes returned later, some wounded and all weary from this unwinnable war, their reception was reserved for thankful family and friends.

The scene of Trooper Butcher's return remains today, though the old wooden bridge has been replaced with one of steel. As one enters the long main street of Whitstable you pass under the railway bridge, not ignored as in many places, but here made a feature of the urban scene. It is painted in 'Whitstable blue' and embellished with the badges of the three railway companies associated with this town.

The railway age in southern England dawned here at Whitstable much earlier with the opening of the steam-operated single-track 'rail road' between the harbour and Canterbury in May 1830[3]. The Stephenson's engine 'Invicta' which worked the end section of the line at Whitstable lasted only six years, thereafter the whole line was operated by cables from fixed engines spaced at intervals. Conversion to locomotive operation only came in 1846. Nevertheless in its early days this line represented the first experiment in the world in the use of steam power to establish a regular service for the transport of goods and passengers. It remained, though, very much a local branch line, mainly concerned with the transport of coal from the harbour to the city, and carrying passengers seeking the sea air and the beach.

Although railway mania had gripped the nation in the 1840s with many lines being constructed, development in Kent was relatively slow since the county lacked large towns and industrial areas. It was not until 1859 that the North Kent Railway began the construction of its main London line from Faversham towards Whitstable.

These railway lines with their embankments, cuttings, tunnels and bridges are now so much part of the landscape that one tends to forget how their construction scarred the countryside and swept away buildings. Routes were mapped, land was purchased, and the tracks pushed through. Here at Whitstable the line crossed the southern end of the main street, involving the removal of the three end cottages of Hartsfield Terrace. A high embankment was needed with a wooden bridge across the road, and the construction of this may explain the moving of the toll-house nearby as described in the previous chapter.

For the designated opening day the bridge works had not been completed and so a temporary platform was erected at the end of Kitchingham Place (now where Clifton Road turns into Portway). This auspicious occasion, August 1st 1860, was described by Sarah Pettman writing to her brother in Australia: 'A grand day on the 1st. instant. On the occasion of the opening of the North Kent Railway from here to Faversham, the streets hung with flags and there was an arch of flags and banners and boughs over the entrance to the new road that leads to the new terminus.'[4]

The Kentish Gazette reported the Directors' inspection on the previous day:

'The party started about three o'clock from Faversham station, and traversing the line in an easy manner, soon arrived at the temporary station at Whitstable, which had been erected a little above the turnpike. A considerable crowd collected at the station, and loudly cheered the train on its arrival.

'The party having alighted, proceeded to view the works for the bridge over the Canterbury road, on one side of which is to be the station, and in which considerable progress has been made.

'This part of the town presented a very gay appearance, the houses, particularly Mr. Maddams, grocer, which had a front ornamented with festoons of flowers and evergreens, exhibiting a profusion of flags, both here and the High Street. The day being fine and the sun shining, imparted a holiday appearance to the town.'[5]

After inspecting progress on the construction of the embankment the directors repaired to the principal hostelry, the Bear and Key, enjoyed 'a cold collation... prepared in elegant style' and then departed by their train to Faversham. Whitstable was now linked directly to the expanding rail network.

The first timetable showed six 'up' trains reaching London in just over

The original Whitstable Station on the bridge

three hours, with a necessary change at Strood on to the South-eastern line. A ticket on the North Kent section cost for each class, four, three and two shillings; day returns were 8/3d., 5/6d., 3/8d. This was therefore a very expensive journey relative to a labourer's weekly wage of ten shillings.

In 1861 the North Kent built its own line into London to a new terminus at Victoria, changing its name to 'London, Chatham and Dover', or popularly, in view of a spate of accidents - 'London, Smash 'em and Turnover'. At Whitstable the station was incorporated in the eastern buttress of the bridge and the wooden platforms extended across the top: '...you went through doors, still there, in the left-hand arch looking towards Canterbury Road, into a booking office and waiting room, then climbed wooden stairs with a metal canopy above, up to the London or Margate side. On the Margate side these stairs went from ground to platform, so homecomers from London could reach the street without going back into the station.'[6]

The railway quickly became popular. Farmers could drive in with their produce and send it directly to London, enlarging their previous limited market. The platform was often stacked high with oyster barrels destined for the capital's ever-expanding demands, from oyster stalls on street corners to the most expensive restaurants. On this prosperity and to meet the market needs the Company in 1886 built the Oyster Stores at the Horsebridge with its storage tanks capable of holding 400,000 oysters.

'The 2/6d excursion was very popular. It opened a new world to those daring enough to take it. People who had only heard of the wonders of London went there themselves to explore. Not many risked the experience of a theatre, which was too sophisticated and smacked of the devil, but historic places were regularly visited, and sometimes the Egyptian Hall where mysteries were presented to a gaping audience, which included some of "our chaps".'

So Fred Goldfinch recounted his 'economical' day visit to London:

'He started with the excursion train, 2/6d. Then he went by underground to the Agricultural Hall, 1/3d. This entitled him to enter the Hall where a Fishery Exhibition was being held. He spent some while studying the display, then had an excellent fish lunch in the restaurant for 6d. Later he had tea there, equally good, for the same price. He had now spent 4/9d. This enabled him to have another cup of tea and a bun on the way home. Thus the whole day, in which he was away from Whitstable for about 15 hours, cost him five shillings.'

The arrival of the main line railway did little to stimulate Whitstable as a residential seaside resort; the town lacked the necessary amenities, especially lodging accommodation. But it did lead to a rapid growth in day excursions. Tankerton beach, the stretch between the harbour and Castle Hill, was much favoured by organisations which viewed the 'resorts' further along the coast as both expensive and a trifle 'sinful'. This was the age of the seaside 'treat', that once-a-year outing for schoolchildren, Sunday School classes, and organisations such as the 'Band of Hope', the Temperance Societies, Bible groups and Friendly Societies. Special trains brought them in their hundreds. Excursion trains on Whit-Monday, the Bank Holiday and Regatta Day saw the beach crowded as 'thousands of visitors streamed into the town, all with the same destination.

'Tankerton Beach was thronged... the booths - gay with new paint outside and plentifully supplied with savoury edibles within - gave abundant

refreshment... Tea and shrimps for eightpence... Boating on a sea as smooth as glass was a leisurely pastime... The Whitstable brass band was of course in action... so there was nothing left to wish for...'[7]

By 1900 agitation for a new railway station was growing in Whitstable. Increasing traffic was producing congestion at the railway bridge and the platforms above were no longer adequate. Where, however, should a new one be built: close to the old town or nearer the developing estates on its eastern side? As has always seemed typical of Whitstable, the town was split in controversy: the railway engineer was said to be 'almost in despair to find unanimity'. In the end the requirements for siting the station really determined its position and it was built where it is today, opening on 2nd January 1915.

After World War One Whitstable began to expand: Tankerton was becoming established; Chestfield village was developing and new roads were appearing off Borstal Hill and Joy Lane. Advertisements presented the attractions of fresh sea air and a quiet small town for those seeking a retirement home, combined with rapid and quick rail transport to the Medway towns and the Metropolis for those remaining at work. Following the Second World War, as house prices closer to London shot up, the town began to spread again, this time mainly westward into Seasalter with estates catering for the railway commuter.

So if one looks at the broad span of Whitstable's history it is apparent that it owes its origin and growth as a town to three aspects of transportation: first by sea, then by road, and more recently by rail. To use the railway bridge as an archway into the town is really most appropriate and the historical connection with the early railway companies is shown by the addition of their badges.

On the left is the seal of the Whitstable to Canterbury Railway, opened in 1830, running between the harbour and the city of Canterbury. This was the first railway line in the world to operate a regular passenger service operated by steam power. When adopted in 1825 the seal showed wagons pulled by horses, for this was the first scheme proposed because of the steeply inclined track. When later it was considered feasible to utilise steam power, the seal was not changed. At the right-hand end is the badge of the South-Eastern Railway which constructed the main line to Whitstable, opening in 1860. The next year, having extended their line into London, to a new terminus at Victoria, the company changed its name to 'London,

The Railwaybridge Today

Chatham and Dover', adopting the badge depicted in the middle of the bridge[8].

The old booking hall, through which Trooper Butcher emerged to such acclaim, and where hundreds of 'Natives' purchased their tickets for the daring visit to the metropolis, this still remains as the town's Labour Club. And it is now electric trains which thunder overhead.

References

1. WT 22.12.1900.
2. Woodman G & G, '**We Remember Whitstable**', Pryor Publications Whitstable 1988, p.7 and following extract p.19.
3. Pike, Page & Cann, 'Ales and Tales: Pubs in the story of Whitstable' Chap 4, '**Sail and Steam**', Whitstable Improvement Trust 1993.
   Hart B, 'The **Canterbury and Whitstable Railway**', Wild Swan Didcot 1991.
4. **Pettman Letters**: 28th August 1860. Whitstable Museum Archive.
5. Kentish Gazette 7.8.1860.
6. Woodman G & G, ref. 2. above, p.7 and following extract pp.19-20.
7. WT 19.5.1883.
8. Pike, Page and Cann, ref 3 above, for the **opening of the railway in 1830**, pp.36-41.
   Pike G, '**Main Line to London, 1860**', Whitstable Improvement Trust 1990, pamphlet.

Tankerton Castle & Seafront circa 1850

8 THE CASTLE AT TANKERTON

The Pearsons at Tankerton Hill

Young Miss Elizabeth Pearson had probably journeyed to 'Tankerton Hill' for several years before the entry in the survivng part of her diary which begins in 1796: 'July 24 left town for Tankerton.'[1] In London she lived in the heart of the city, above the shop where her father Charles had his glover's business. This connection with Tankerton had come about through her mother, who, as Elizabeth Radford, had inherited part of the old-established copperas works there. After her marriage to Charles Pearson in 1780, he bought up the remaining works, becoming sole owner of the small industrial area. This moved Charles socially from trade into manufacturing, but his real aim was to establish himself as a country gentleman at Tankerton. When the opportunity came in the early 1790s he purchased the

adjoining estate of St Anne's Barn farm of some 140 acres: he also bought the title of 'Lord of the Manor of Whitstable'[2].

By the mid-1790s the Pearson family would spend some three months each year at Tankerton. They journeyed down by chaise towards the end of July and remained until late October, the party consisting of Mrs Pearson (also Elizabeth), the eldest daughter the diarist Elizabeth, son Charles and the two younger girls Clara and Amelia. Charles Senior might sometimes travel with them, either in the chaise or alongside on horseback. It was a lengthy and tiring journey on the roads of the day, so the horses were changed at Dartford and at Sittingbourne, and this provided an opportunity for the appropriate meals. Indeed they often stayed the night, travelling either way, at the Rose Inn at Sittingbourne. An early start, however, enabled the journey to be completed in one day: (1798) 'started at 8 for Tankerton arrived at 7'.

THE TANKERTON COPPERAS INDUSTRY

The knobbly nodules of copperas, one of the mineral forms of iron sulphate, occur naturally in the local London clay. Due in particular to cliff recession these were found prolifically as part of the local beach material stretching some distance off-shore. Some may still be found today along the shingle bank, the 'Street'. From the mineral, by a rather primitive chemical process, crystals of ferrous sulphate, 'green vitriol', were produced. These were exported from jetties below the cliffs for sale in London

On being dissolved the crystals formed a black liquid used in various industrial processes: leather tanning; as a constituent in black ink and dye; as part of lime-wash and distemper, and in sheep dressings. Most especially it was required as the fixing agent or mordant essential in the use of natural dyes for cotton and woollen materials so that they would remain colour-fast. Until chemical dyes were introduced in the early nineteenth century copperas was widely collected and processed in plants along the Thames estuary. At first the nodules were simply collected up, but later the foreshore was raked to produce larger quantities.

One Cornelius Stephenson was granted a Royal Patent to exploit the mineral at Tankerton in 1565 as he had 'first found out means to use certain goldstones, otherwise sulphur stones, which were gathered in the beach'. Within 50 years six copperas processing works had been established, and later eighteenth century sale records show that they were regarded as valuable acquisitions.

For processing, the nodules (chemically iron pyrites) were gathered into piles and allowed to weather; a process assisted by dowsing them with water. Then the decaying mass was shovelled into long trenches lined with beaten clay (called copperas beds or pannels) with layers interspersed with quantities of small bits of iron such as filings. Oxidation produced sulphuric acid which further assisted the chemical reduction. The resulting liquid was drained off into lead pans where it was boiled for some days, more iron being added to absorb the sulphuric acid. The concentrated liquid was then run off into lead vats, 'coolers', in which the crystals would gradually form on bundles of birch twigs. The main processing was carried out inside a building known as a copperas house. For the man in charge there was usually a dwelling house attached. When Charles Pearson became sole owner he installed a manager, Thomas Porter, in one of the houses; this was later enlarged as the North Lodge of Tankerton Tower. This last relic of the copperas industry was demolished in 1960 to make way for a car park.

With the sulphurous smell from the copperas, first decomposing and then being boiled, the dumps of coal and the smoke from the boilers, and the carrying of the green vitriol down to the jetties, this part of the coastline - amazing as it seems today - must have presented all the smells, noise and grime of an industrial area.

References

1. Map - detail of The Copperas 'houses: see the Oyster Map of 1770, p. 42.
2. George W, 'A Forgotten Industry - Aspects of the **Copperas Industry in SE England**', thesis, University of Kent, ref. 093/F72748.
3. Goodsall RH, 'The **Whitstable Copperas Industry**', AC v. LXX 1956 p.142.
4. Original deeds in '**Tankerton Estate Deeds 1598-1919**', Kent Archives Office ref. U905.
5. Page W, Ed. '**Victoria County History of Kent**'. St Catharine's Press 1932, v.3 p.397.

Where, then, did they spend these three months at 'Tankerton Hill' as Elizabeth called it? Probably in 1789 Charles Pearson built a tower in the fashionable 'Gothic' style of the day: it still survives at the 'The Castle' as the centre of the east front. This must have been attached to some other building, but, alas, as so often, the diary is short on such background information. All Elizabeth gives is one note: (1798) 'The hall chimney has been taken down and a staircase made in its place.' It seems the house was known as Tankerton Farm' and after Charles' purchase of the manorial title, 'Manor Hall' (1797). It may well have been a surviving part of an ancient manor house to which the addition of a battlemented tower would not have looked incongruous[3]. The house would certainly have faced east for not far away on the other side were the grimy and smelly copperas works, though the nearest had been pulled down and its bricks used in constructing the tower.

Life at Tankerton, as in London, revolved around the routine of daily meals: breakfast, dinner in the early afternoon, tea - essentially a cup or two as a social custom - and then supper later in the evening. To assist the family the cook and parlour maid were sent down by hoy[4] to Whitstable several days in advance of the family's arrival. 'Taking tea' was the occasion for social visits, although opportunities for this were much more limited here than in London for such exchanges of courtesy were limited to the appropriate social level. At Tankerton only the Vicar and the Hyders of Court Lees seemed to be recognized. On Sundays church attendance took much of the day, the family either attending both All Saints and St John the Baptist at Swalecliffe, or dividing their attendance between them: presumably considered judicious for the 'Lord of the Manor'.

There were often one or two friends from London staying with the family and much time was spent in walking the local area. On her way to the Parsonage on August 5th in 1797 Elizabeth noted that she visited 'Trollop Fair'. This was the ancient dredgermen's fair held on Old St James' Day by the 'Two Brewers Inn'. What reputation, one wonders, did she mean by this expression? On another occasion they made their return walk by 'Borstol Hill over the crooked hedge field'. Another walk noted was past Whitstable as far as 'Bunce's saltworks now abandoned.'[5] The sea figures rarely in the diary entries: in one (September 1799) 'Very fine all 9 on the sea.' and in 1804 'Father and Charles and Mr March went fishing took little Tom Porter to carry the basket brought home a few roach.'[6]

There were occasional excitements: in the autumn of 1798 there is

recorded 'The Duke of Manchester, Ld Inchingbrook and the Huntingdon Militia at Whitstable'. Did Elizabeth admire some fine young men? Then on October 8th 'Whitstable illuminated for Nelson's victory'. In the early October of 1804 the fuller details for a short stay in Canterbury suggest the enjoyment of this break from the rather routine life at Tankerton. This season, too, there was an additional companion, another young girl, Mary Smith, a cousin and an orphan child of a former business partner of Charles Pearson. Elizabeth with Charles and Clara walked over to Canterbury from Tankerton to stay with Mrs Johnson the recent widow of the Vicar of Whitstable. Charles, though, stayed at the Fountain Inn, probably because there were only ladies in the house. The girls attended service at the cathedral and on the next day went out to the 'old park' beyond St Augustine's to see the 'Scotch Grays' exercising, and on their way back they visited the Master's Gardens in the Close and the Dunghill (now the Danejohn). Much time was taken with calling on acquaintances of Mrs Johnson and doubtless consuming many cups of tea.

On the Wednesday the young people walked 'to Harbledown and back a

very delightful walk, a beautiful romantic little village.' Charles, who had been sketching there, returned with them, came in for cake, and then set off with a friend for Sturry. The ladies however remained as Elizabeth recorded: 'Returned. Dined. Tea.' The following day the party returned home, 'the weather being wet were taken up in a post chaise... and returned to Whitstaple much pleased with our jaunt.'

The surviving part of Elizabeth's diary does not resume until 1820; sixteen years have passed and the writer is now a mature young woman. Her entries have become fuller and her observations have a greater range: there are now descriptive comments on the weather and the sea. Then, too, the family are older - young Charles is married and producing an ever-increasing family - and it is noticeable that they lead a much more varied and affluent way of life: they travel and stay in hotels. This change was doubtless brought about by the death of their mother Elizabeth in 1817. She appears to have been very thrifty for in London the girls were always busily engaged in mending and adapting their clothes. One suspects, too, that she did not have a close, warm relationship with her family: she rarely appears in Elizabeth's jottings. By 1820 young Charles had been allowed his head and the girls could easily manage their father.

The house at 'Tankerton Hill' was now about to undergo its first major development: young Charles, with the assistance of a Mr Inman, was planning to build a new block adjoining his father's tower. Charles had great social pretensions and needed also to accommodate his growing family - there were now five children. So in 1820 Elizabeth recorded much coming and going from their London home by Charles, and in June she came over from Ramsgate with her father and Clara to inspect the house. They now travelled by steamship: she notes 'Returned home by the London Engineer. Had a delightful voyage'.

In July young Charles took a house for three months in Herne Bay and had the furniture from Tankerton moved there while the building work was in progress. Here, in addition to the usual round of social visits, the family enjoyed some of the pleasures of the rising seaside resort. They made an expedition to Herne in a donkey chaise with two riding separate donkeys and Elizabeth had taken to sea-bathing. In June she recorded a visit to Whitstable in a 'barouche' and wrote 'I bathed in the sea and Clara took a warm Bath.' The bath was a tank of heated sea water for those who found the sea a little chilly or perhaps a little daunting. Advertisements show that the very necessary bathing machine had been available for some years at Whitstable[7]. Next month at Herne Bay she expressed disappointment: 'Sea too rough to bathe. Walked along shore. Rain and Wind.' And on returning to London in September Elizabeth rather proudly recorded 'Bathed at Hearn Bay 15 times at Whitstable 4 times.'

For Thursday 10th August (1820) the diary records: 'The first brick is now laid.' Young Charles' addition to the original tower was depicted in an engraving for a Thanet Guide, probably published in 1828[8]. It shows how the battlemented style was maintained, although the window details were now in the current fashion for Tudor. Facing the main east front a garden had been laid out (are those just conventional figures depicted in the engraving or might they be members of the Pearson family?) The building work was completed within the year for in September 1821 Charles brought his wife and children with their nursemaid to the new house. A little later they were joined by Elizabeth and her father from Ramsgate where they had been enjoying a seaside holiday: 'Amelia and I rode beyond Pegwell Bay in a Donkey Curricle.' and 'All took a drive to Sandwich in an open carriage. Saw the remains of Richborough Castle.'[9]

At Tankerton Elizabeth continued her usual occupations: 'Bathed in sea 2nd time', 'Bathed. Walked from breakfast till dinner.' and even 'Bathed before breakfast.' She obviously relished her walks: 'Showery. Scarcely got out.' But the next day she was not deterred, she wrote 'Showery. Walked to the Marine Barracks by Whitstable.'[10]

In early November, by varying routes and conveyances the members of the Pearson family returned to London and here the surviving second section of Elizabeth's diary ends. However tantalising this is, for there are troubles ahead, enough has remained to provide some acquaintance with the first occupants of the house at 'Tankerton Hill'.

Wynn Ellis and Tankerton Tower

The story of the house now moves to 1836, to a new owner, but many connections with the Pearson family continue. 'Tankerton Tower' as the property is now called, has been purchased by Wynn Ellis, a London draper and silk importer. His wife is the Mary Smith, the orphan girl in the care of Charles Pearson, and who, in 1804, Elizabeth noted as visiting Tankerton. Wynn Ellis has been acquainted with the Pearsons for some twenty years from shortly after his arrival in London in 1812 at the age of 22. He shared with Charles Pearson Senior a common background in Northamptonshire and both were engaged in the hosiery trade. Charles, indeed, may well have helped the young man who arrived in the city, as he himself had done, to make a career and hopefully his fortune. Wynn Ellis quickly established himself not far from the Pearsons, in Ludgate Street, presumably in partnership with an established business. How, one wonders, did he acquire the necessary finance so quickly, for his father is recorded simply as a coachman. Within two years he had married Mary Maria; was there perhaps some financial advantage in the match? Such circumstances would have been understood, even perhaps encouraged by Charles, for he himself had married a much older woman, a lady of property. This motive of personal advantage is made delightfully clear by Elizabeth in an 1804 diary entry relating to London friends: 'As Joseph Fabian is going to be a Stock Broker recommended him to pay court to Miss Pickles as I hear she

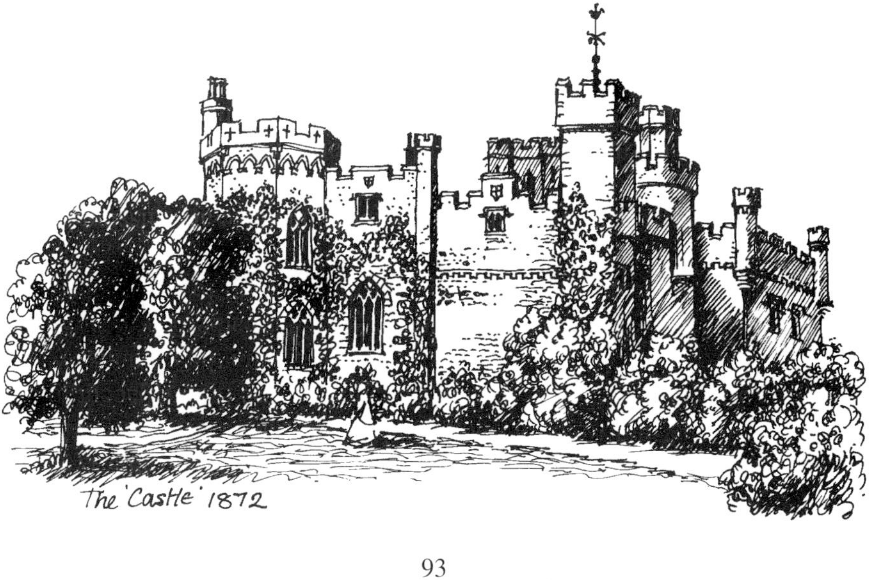

is a nice girl and is the only daughter of a Stock Broker.' Charles Pearson may also have sensed a good future prospect for his niece in a young man whose capacity for hard work, drive and business acumen must have been apparent early on, judging by the speed with which his career prospered.

Wynn Ellis in later life

The sale of the Tower to Wynn Ellis was brought about by the acute financial difficulties of Charles Pearson Junior, and his resulting bankruptcy in 1835 for £14,000. An extravagant standard of living and imprudent business investments were to blame. Locally he had invested in the steam operated rail-road between Whitstable and Canterbury, opened in 1830. He also built an hotel 'The Pearson's Arms' on the edge of the Tower ground to serve travellers on the line, but it was unsuitably situated and was not a financial success. From 1832 the now wealthy Wynn Ellis gradually bought out some of Charles' mortgages, and in this way, by 1836, he was owner of the Tower and had purchased the manorial title of Whitstable. As Steward he appointed Charles Hill Pearson, eldest son of Charles Junior, who also worked for him in London.

As one judges from the character of Wynn Ellis personal advantage was well to the fore in any financial matters. At least initially his acquisition of Tankerton Tower was not so much a desire for a country seat as a need for a rural retreat. It was not Mary Maria, his wife, whom he brought to live at the Tower but his mistress of some years, Susan Lloyd. Family tradition has it that Mary either would not, or could not, bear children and so by 1836 there was a daughter and in that year a son by Susan Lloyd. Clearly there could not have been any secrecy about this arrangement; such an accommodation to circumstances was perfectly acceptable in Victorian society provided it was handled with due discretion.

Wynn Ellis was now in his forties; he was a wealthy man and a public figure. His silk importing and retail business was centred at 1-3 St Paul's Churchyard, at the centre of London's haberdashery and drapers' trade. In 1839 he was due to be proposed as Alderman when friends persuaded him to seek a political career instead; he stood and was elected MP for the borough of Leicester. That year, 1836, seems to have been the turning point from his business career to that of public figure: in addition to Tankerton and his house in fashionable Cadogan Square as a town residence, he also purchased the Manor of Ponsbourne Park in Hertfordshire as his country seat.

How exactly the domestic arrangement was managed we do not know of course. But Susan was properly recognised: a Deed of Settlement of 1845 gave her and her daughter Susan Olinda a life interest in the Tower and all the surrounding estate amounting to 327 acres of farmland. Further purchases were added between 1847 and 1851, including the windmill on Borstal Hill (the subject of Chapter Ten). Susan is named as living at 27 Oxford Terrace, Hyde Park, so she had her town home as well[11]. It is likely that at this time, as indeed it has always been, the Tower was used only as a summer residence by the sea.

The Tithe map of 1842[12] shows that the house had not changed since the addition of 1820 and the grounds, termed 'shrubbery', are of limited extent. The land on the west is still named 'copperas beds', but its use is recorded as 'pasture'; all buildings have been removed. It was probably towards 1850 that Wynn Ellis decided to make major improvements to the Tower and its surroundings; he may have felt the need in his social life for a suitable seaside residence. He added a long west front to the existing building, overlooking gardens landscaped by Dr Alexander Garry, a noted plant collector in Far Eastern countries. The well-known plant named after him, *Garrya Elliptica,* is said to have first been planted in England at the Tower.

The east front was extended in a somewhat baronial style with a large clock and bell tower; doubtless the large oriental bell was obtained by Dr Garry. The castellated style of the original building was maintained with rusticated stonework, battlements and a number of towers. 'Tankerton Tower' was now dignified with proper entrances. On the south side an avenue of trees led down to a lodge on the road to Church Street, and another driveway ran westward to the main entrance leading to Whitstable; here there was a large lodge-cum-stables and coachman's house. On the north side the old Copperas Manager's house was occupied by the gardener.

The 1841 enumerator's census returns for Whitstable are missing so the establishment at that time is unknown. That for 1861 is most interesting, for resident are Wynn Ellis and his wife Mary Maria, together with cook, parlour-maid, and coachman. The servants' places of birth indicate that they had been brought from the Hertfordshire house[13]. Then there is a venerable head gardener aged 89 and an under gardener and his wife occupying the coach-house. Wynn Ellis and his wife are now turned 70 and one may speculate how often Mary Maria had visited Tankerton since her visits with the Pearson family. Then there were the children: did they always live with their mother until her death in 1869? Susan Olinda was apparently delicate; Arthur studied at Oxford and entered the Church - at some stage his name was changed to Graystone. In his will Wynn Ellis left the very large sum of £50,000 to be paid to five Reverend gentlemen two years after his death: was this in recompense for undertaking some kind of guardianship of the young Arthur Wynn Graystone?

The extent to which Wynn Ellis involved himself in Whitstable affairs is difficult to estimate until the commencement of the Whitstable Times in 1864. In the early years building up his London business and other financial dealings, and then his political career, must have absorbed most of his energies and time. With his official seat in Hertfordshire, that county became the centre of his personal life: he became a magistrate and in 1851 was honoured with selection as Sheriff of the county. For some two years from 1843 Wynn Ellis did serve as a member of the Trustees of the Whitstable Charities. This may well have been due to his feeling as Lord of the Manor that he should be involved in the planning and building of the St Alphege Church and the Charity School (now the 'Endowed'). These were, of course, major developments which marked Whitstable's transition from village to town[14]. He was also appointed a magistrate in Kent.

It was in his later years that Wynn Ellis demonstrated an attachment for Tankerton Tower. By the 1860s together with his wife he may well have adopted the custom of spending the summer months there. In 1864 he presided at the manorial Court Leet and dinner, and in 1867 similarly at the Court Baron, the first time for some years it was noted by the Whitstable Times. In July 1865 a 'Grand Pic-Nic' was held in the field adjacent to the house and two weeks later another of these was held in the grounds. When a disastrous fire swept through the largely tarred weatherboard buildings west of the harbour in Whitstable he contributed £100 to the final Relief

Fund of £800. However, in that year a certain caution is evident when approached for a contribution towards the building of a new Infant School (St Alphege). He replied that normally he was 'compelled owing to the pressure on me for aid from all quarters to restrict myself to places where I reside'. The new school would actually be sited in the Parish of Seasalter although in reality it would serve a large section of the town. This Wynn Ellis grudgingly accepted: 'place me as a subscriber for £20,' he replied and he duly laid the foundation stone in 1865[15].

Reaching the age of 80 in 1870, and although remaining vigorous both in health and in mind, Wynn Ellis seems to have reflected on his life and contemplated its end.

First he set about converting the old 'Pearson's Arms', long closed and from 1850 used as a Coastguard Station, into an almshouse providing twelve apartments for elderly people. On the central gable was placed a tablet inscribed 'These almshouses were erected to the Memory of Dame Mary Maria Ellis 1873'. The following year he contributed £400 to the restoration of All Saints Church, with a typical rider that he would give £200 more if the Appeal Fund reached £800. He also gave one and half acres of ground to extend the churchyard on the north side. As always with Wynn Ellis one sees some personal motive, for this space was to be dominated by a massive mausoleum, said to have cost £900. Designed by Edward Middleton Barry, son of Charles the architect of the Houses of Parliament, its monumental design was constructed in the finest Portland stone; the vault was entered through massive oak doors with bronze embellishments, and inside under a cupola was a floor in red and white Mansfield stone bordered with black marble. In August 1875 the body of Mrs Ellis was brought from Hatfield and reinterred in this grand family mausoleum. Some seventy years had passed since those days when the youthful Mary Maria stayed with her cousins at 'Tankerton Hill'.

In September 1875 Wynn Ellis presided at Whitstable's annual Regatta, supporting the event with prizes. Then in little over a month this extraordinary life ended.

'In the early part of November, 1875, Mr Ellis left Whitstable, to spend the winter at his town residence in Cadogan Place, and on the 20th of the same month, without any intermission of illness, and in full possession of his faculties, he died. Throughout his whole life he had enjoyed unbroken good health, and his death even at the advanced age of 85 was totally unexpect-

ed; the machine was not worn out by sickness, it was still in perfect order, but suddenly the springs of life stood still, and the spirit "was not" here.

'His mortal remains were conveyed to Whitstable by special train from London accompanied by the chief friends and relatives of the deceased gentleman: on arriving the train was met by those invited to attend the funeral... also Mr Ellis's tentants, stewards, and gardener at Tankerton. The funeral cortege consisted of a hearse decked with plumes, and drawn by four horses, and seven mourning coaches... the mournful procession passed through the town where the shops closing without exception, evidenced the prevailing respect felt for the late Lord of the Manor.'[16] (WJ Cox, Editor, Whitstable Times)

So passed away the most distinguished and wealthy man to have been associated with Whitstable: his fortune was made in the city of London, but it was here that he chose to be buried. He died a self-made millionaire and a man very typical of his age in personal character and entrepreneurial skill together with immense industry. He left not only an estate worth £600,000 but also a huge art collection which contributed major paintings to the National Gallery collection. No less than £125,000 was left to charities: most of the bequests went to institutions serving the needs of children - to promote education, to help those who were afflicted or in great poverty. Amongst the lengthy list was the Oundle Parochial Schools where this coachman's son began his own education[17].

One must wonder if this concern for the needs of children reflected a sadness in his own life, for at his funeral one of the participating clergy was the Revd. Arthur Graystone, the son who could not carry forward his father's name.

The Graystones at the Castle

Obituary notices for Wynn Ellis refer to his residence as Tankerton Tower, but WJ Cox, proprietor and Editor of the Whitstable Times, commissioned an engraving in 1872 which is entitled 'Tankerton Castle, the Seat of Wynn Ellis Esq.', and it was this name that was used by the succeeding owners: his daughter, son and grandson.

Miss Susan Ellis continued the tradition of spending each summer at Tankerton. She apparently disliked living alone in the large house and so had the coach-house at the west gate converted into a rather charming cottage, now called Albion Cottage.

Miss Ellis, as Lady of the Manor, took an interest in the town and allowed fetes to be held in the Castle grounds. After a long illness she died in 1884. She was not buried in the family mausoleum at All Saints, but alongside her mother at the Kensal Green Cemetery[18].

All the Tankerton property now passed to her brother, the Revd. Arthur Graystone; perhaps the only millionaire vicar? Again he was a summer resident, and he, too, continued the family involvement with the town. Through him the Graystone Freemason Lodge was established in Whitstable. Like his sister he suffered from ill-health and died at his London home in Lancaster Gate in 1886. His burial, however, was in the Ellis Mausoleum at All Saints Church[19].

So after only fourteen years the elder grandson of Wynn Ellis, Sydney Wynn Graystone became owner of the Tankerton estate and the manorial title. He was aged 24 and not long down from Cambridge. Now it seemed as though the family connection might prevail for many years. The young man had joined the local cricket club and together with his brother Herbert was a keen yachtsman and had competed in the Regatta. In 1888 he was unanimously proposed and duly elected as the Councillor for Whitstable on the newly established Kent County Council[20]. Yet in 1890 the whole estate was sold and Sydney Graystone departed for Somerset; no mention of this decision occurs in the local paper: the matter is ignored.

The Tankerton Estate Company and Tankerton Towers

The purchaser of the Castle and estate was a London barrister Charles Newton Robinson, undoubtedly with development planned with two associates: barrister and businessman Edward Bond and the distinguished architect Basil Champneys. On 2nd July 1890 the private Tankerton Estate Company was incorporated with a capital of £25,000[21]. The intention, as their brochure declared, was 'The complete development of this magnificent property as a new seaside Watering Place of the first class... now for the first time Tankerton has been opened up to the public, there seems the highest probability that its beauty and advantages will be appreciated, and its success immediate and assured.' An outline plan was published showing a grid pattern of parallel roads leading to wide boulevards with the Marine Parade overlooking the bay; there was the 'Kingsdown' Park, sites for rows of shops and a number of hotels. Tankerton was to be a miniature Eastbourne on the north Kent coast.

To match the pretentiousness of the scheme the Auction Sales were launched in an extravagant manner in June 1891. The initial plan for 'The Towers' (a more appropriate country house name it was thought) was to sell it with the grounds extending to the cliffs overlooking the sea, at a price of £10,000. Unfortunately for this fledgling company the 1890s were years of economic depression and no offers were received. Leasing was then offered but after some inconclusive negotiations it was decided in 1892 to reduce the grounds of 'the Towers', setting back the entrance gate so that a new road could be constructed curving round on the north side of the house, providing more building plots on the seaward side. For a period of six months in 1895 'the Towers' was let to the then celebrated dramatist Arthur Wing Pinero, one of a number of theatrical folk who have found Whitstable an attractive haven (see Chapter Ten).

In 1896 the new road was developed and two large houses built, and to the east land was sold to the brewers Mackesons as a site for the Tankerton Hotel. The splendid situation of Wynn Ellis's residence by the sea was now considerably reduced as commercial development emerged on all sides. The company, becoming desperate for money, offered 'the Towers' for sale at £4000 and in July 1897 it was sold to Mr Thomas Edward Adams for £3,250.

The Towers' as a Country House

Mr Adams enhanced the property with a handsome west gatehouse; he died in 1902 and the following year Mrs Adams married Mr Noel Argent Pell and it remained in their possession until 1920. Little information is available as to life at the house during these years. It seems probable that summer occupation continued and there were various social events held which opened up the grounds to the public.

In 1920 the house was bought by Mr Albert Mallandain, a paper manufacturer. He also purchased from Mrs Newton Robinson the title of Lord of the Manor of Whitstable for this has no direct connection with ownership of the property.

Mr Mallandain appointed a Steward and occasionally held the Manor Court, the last person to do so, although by now this was little more than an occasion to hold a dinner.

Mr Mallandain lived at 'The Towers' during the summer months and entertained a great deal; there were frequent weekend house parties and their annual garden party was the social event of the Whitstable calendar[22].

It is a happy coincidence for this, the final phase of today's 'Castle' as a home, that there are available the recollections of a young woman who lived there - but this time, in contrast to Elizabeth Pearson, from 'below stairs'[23]. Kate was nineteen when she came to join the staff in 1924 as a housemaid. As often happened in domestic service, this was by way of a family recommendation: her cousin was kitchen maid. There was also a parlour maid and all worked under the direction of cook-housekeeper Mrs Warner.

Life as a housemaid, she recalled, was poorly paid: £2 a month with 'all found' as the saying went, and she was allowed one half day off each week. Her day would start at around 5.30 a.m. as the junior making tea for the staff. First there was a round of cleaning the grates and the lighting of the fires; the shoes left outside bedrooms by the guests; next the main rooms, hall and stairs - and all to be in order before the master and mistress came down, although this was a little easier if breakfast was carried upstairs to their bedroom. If there were guests Kate would help the parlour maid to serve breakfast before moving on to the making of beds and tidying bedrooms. After assisting with lunch she would be carrying logs to the various fireplaces and polishing brass and silver in the basement, and later carrying food and drinks to the reception rooms as required. The 'Towers; as it was known to her, was a most inconvenient establishment with many different levels linked by stairs. Life there involved much carrying to and fro and running up and down.

The Mallandains occupied the house between June and September and enjoyed entertaining with weekend house-parties. How pleasant it must have been to enter their elegantly furnished home by the entrance lobby into the panelled hall with its large grandfather clock and bright bowl of flowers freshly picked from the garden. The stairs led down to the drawing room with tapestried walls and a log fire burning; there were upholstered window seats so that guests could look out into the beautiful gardens or in the evening listen to their hostess play on her grand piano. From this room one could stroll through into the large conservatory with its central marble statue and small fountain, all surrounded by a splendid collection of tropical plants.

Leading off the hall to the right was the octagon-shaped dining room lit with a splendid chandelier (this was in Charles Pearson's original tower). There was a small electric dumb-waiter installed but for dinner parties Kate would often be running up and down the stairs bringing dishes from the kitchen.

Beyond the dining room there was the new wing added by Mr Mallandain which contained on the ground floor a splendidly panelled room with an ornate fireplace and tapestried chairs grouped around the central billiard table. Here guests would often gather in the evening after dinner for coffee to be served.

Ascending the carved oak stairs one came to the main bedrooms, and to the right the master bedroom, octagon shaped in the tower and like the dining room below, having an ornate plaster frieze with curious heads running round the base of the ceiling. The servants, of course, used the separate back stairs leading to bedrooms over the billiard room; the maids shared in pairs and the housekeeper had her own room.

When the Mallandains were in residence a flag was raised from the clock tower and each week a man called to wind the heavy clock mechanism. In the early twenties when Mr Mallandain still went to his office he would often walk down to the railway station. One of the young gardeners would open the lodge gates for him at six o'clock and then close them on his return at the end of the day. If wet the chauffeur would have the Rolls Royce waiting. The extensive gardens and greenhouses were maintained by a Head Gardener and three assistants; flowers and vegetables were required at the house each day. In the lower ground there was an extensive kitchen garden and beyond that poultry were kept. There were tennis courts to maintain and there was a large summer house which was turned during the day to follow the sun. As indoors, there was a never-ending round of tasks to be done. However, outside and inside staff did meet - perhaps in country house style for an early kitchen lunch - for Kate became fond of one of the young under-gardeners and in 1929 became Mrs Kate Anderson. The young couple were provided with accommodation in the North Lodge, the last relic of the copperas industry.

Trusteeship of the the almshouses had been conveyed to Mr Mallandain and he and his wife took a great interest in the elderly residents, employing a resident nurse to care for them. Each year he organised an outing by coach with a tea-party at some attractive spot, but the highlight of the year was the summer Garden Party to which they were invited to join the house-guests and those fortunate enough to be invited from the town. The company sat along the terrace overlooking the wide sweep of the splendid gardens and were served with delicious refreshments while being entertained by the resident group from the 'Lawn Pavilion' (opposite the nearby Tankerton Hotel)

- Mr 'Radio' Willie Rouse and his Bohemian Concert Party. Kate remembered these as most enjoyable occasions in spite of all the hard work involved.

After 1932 Mr Mallandain, now in his eighties, no longer came to Tankerton and two years later he decided not to retain the house. Kate and her husband moved to Surrey where they lived for a couple of years before returning to Whitstable to settle in Church Street, running a small market garden. Widowed in 1970, Kate Anderson became a resident herself in the Wynn Ellis Almshouses.

Epilogue

Mr Mallandain offered the 'Towers' to the local Urban District Council to use for their meetings and as offices. After much debate and haggling over the price the purchase was agreed at £10,500. His affection for Whitstable was expressed in the presentation of a splendid gold chain-of-office for the Council Chairman[24], and much later, in 1953, when the town was overwhelmed by the sea he donated £1000 to the relief fund.

So Whitstable gained a dignified council chamber (the former billiard room) and to extend the office accommodation a flat roofed extension was added to 'The Castle', replacing the conservatory. The grounds became the town's only public park: the tennis courts, now the rose garden, were converted into an enclosure for dancing and summer shows. A bowling green was laid on the kitchen garden area. With government reorganisation in 1972 the council was abolished and all the departments moved to Canterbury. The future of the building seemed very uncertain. Happily the Whitstable Society demonstrated it had a practical and much needed use as a centre for community activities and it now operates as 'The Castle Centre Association'.

The building flourishes all the year round as a meeting place for all manner of local societies and groups, and here, too, townsfolk celebrate engagements, weddings and birthdays. The attractive grounds are still to be enjoyed and each year the crowds gather for the May Day celebrations. What was once so privately preserved has now become open to all. There is talk, as in all old buildings with odd rooms and darkened corners, of a ghostly female figure fleetingly glimpsed - which of the ladies in the story of 'The Castle' might this be, one wonders?

References

1. **Elizabeth Pearson's diary** is owned by a descendant of the Pearson family: it survives for 1796-1805 and 1820-22 - copy in the Whitstable Museum archive.
2. For the **sale of the Manor of Whitstable in 1791** see conclusion of Chapter Four.
3. Goodsall RH, '**Whitstable, Seasalter and Swalecliffe** - the History of Three Kent Parishes', Canterbury 1938, discusses the location of a 'Tankerton Farm'. There were certainly several important houses somewhere in Tankerton: wealthy landowner Henry Crisp listed 'my house at Tankerton' in his will, 1575 AC v. XXXI 1926, p.51; and Thomas Alen or Aleyne lived at the 'Downe', Tankerton, 1523 (Goodsall, ref. above p.147).
4. A hoy was a sailing vessel of shallow draught much used in coastal waters.
5. Cyprian Rondeau **Bunce** was a Canterbury solicitor and antiquarian. In 1794 he enclosed some thirteen acres of the foreshore in front of the recently built Island Wall for the making of '**Bay Salt**'. The business lasted only a few years, being abandoned by 1799. It was advertised for sale in 1801 but there is no evidence of its continuation. Details in the Manor Roll of Whitstable 28.10.1795 (Whitstable Museum Wallace Harvey collection and Goodsall, ref. 3 above p.31.
6. **Thomas Porter** of Canterbury came to Tankerton as Manager of the Copperas Works in the early 1790s and lived in the house which became known later as North Lodge. He probably started what became the family building business in 1829 and this may well indicate that the copperas industry had petered out by that time.
7. Goodsall RH, ref. 3 above, details the early history of sea-bathing at Whitstable.

stle today - West front

8. Blackmantle B, 'Merry Guide to Margate, Ramsgate and Broadstairs', George Herbert London c.1828 - **Tankerton Tower engraved** by J and HS Storer. Published as Plate XXVII facing p.213 in Goodsall RH, ref. 3 above.
9. Whyman J, 'The **Early Kentish Seaside**', Kentish Sources VIII, Kent Archives 1985: details the broader background.
10. 'Barracks' - Elizabeth probably means an **Excise Post** - those in which confiscated goods were stored were certainly substantial and well guarded buildings.
11. Details of the **purchase of Tankerton Tower by Wynn Ellis** in 'Abstract of Title - 1890 for the Tankerton Estate Company' and 'Deed of Settlement 1845': Deeds for the Castle, Tankerton held by Canterbury City Council. A longer 'Abstract of Title' in Kent Archives, D1724, pt. 1.
12. **Tithe Map of Whitstable Parish**: Canterbury Cathedral Archives.
13. **Census 1861**, enumerator's returns: microfilm Canterbury City Library.
14. Minutes of the Trustees of **Whitstable Charities 1844-50**, Whitstable Museum, Wallace Harvey collection.
15. '**St Alphege - Centenary Year** (1875-1975)', booklet (Wallace Harvey for the School) p.2.
16. **Cox WJ, 'Guide** to Whitstable and its surroundings', Whitstable 1876: Almshouses p.12-14; Churchyard and Mausoleum p.14.
17. The **life of Wynn Ellis** is more fully described in Pike G, 'The Story of Copperas and the Castle', Whitstable Improvement Trust booklet n/d; Dictionary of National Biography; Obituary in the Times 25.11.1875; biography and details of the art collection in Illustrated London News (Wills and Bequests) 8.1.1876; sale of London properties in Times 27.4.1876.
18. WT 24.11.1877 and 10.5.1884 (**Susan Ellis**).
19. WT 3.8.1886. (**Rev. Arthur Graystone**).
20. WT 24.11.1888. (**Sydney Wynn Graystone**).
21. WT 6.9.1890. The early land sales and **development of Tankerton** are described in Pike G, Page M, Cann J, 'Ales and Tales - pubs in the story of Whitstable', Whitstable Improvement Trust 1993 Chapter 10 'A Place for Wealth and Health'.
22. WT 27.7.1925
23. Tape **recording of Kate Anderson** made in 1977 by Mr J Bird and held by Mrs K Williamson. Biographical article in WT 15.4.1977.
24. WT 13.4.1935 (Chairman's chain of office); 26.4.1935 (negotiations for purchase); 1.12.1956 .

Cottages along Island Wall and the old 'Favourite' Oyster Smack on its original site.

9 THE 'FAVOURITE' OYSTER SMACK

It was quite a typical scene on the beach fronting Island Wall that fine September morning in 1952, as men and muscle gathered to effect the moving of the Favourite, one of the few surviving Whitstable oyster dredgers. She lay on the beach by the old slipway of Collar's shipyard and indeed the smack had been built just over 60 years previously further along at the yard of John Dyason.

Many craft before her had occupied a similar position: drawn up on the beach for repair or 'blacking' and then returned for service at sea. That day's activity was, however, a little different, for the task in hand was to pull the Favourite landward: to give her a final resting place on Island Wall.

Henry Hurford Janes, whose cottage overlooked the part of the beach, had decided to organise a rescue, for there was talk of breaking up the old vessel. Another of his instincts had also forced him into action: 'the same

instinct that resulted in him wobbling along on bicycles laden with pieces of four-poster bed or spending hours exploring the dusty depths of junk shops to emerge triumphant with a bargain or two... "I just have to rescue and conserve things" he said'[1].

'Another reason was that in her span of three score years and ten, the Favourite had seen more history than one would expect in a modest fishing vessel designed to dredge for oysters in a sheltered bay.

'For ten years, the Favourite had lain on the beach, an uncomfortable berth for a craft usually anchored offshore when not working. In her early days she was one of the comeliest ships that ever dredged those valuable Whitstable oyster beds, or, on less official duty, brought brandy and tobacco for smugglers. Yes, she could turn her tiller to any account according to the requirements of Billingsgate or for that matter anyone making it worth her while. "She's earned more gold," said one ancient mariner with more

than a touch of Coleridge, "than she could carry in 'er 'old." As she carried eight tons of iron ballast over and above her catch, this would amount to a tidy sum.

'But those were the glories that belong to the days when a hundred and fifty ships put to sea on a single tide. Today, no yawls dredge for oysters off Whitstable...

'It would be hard to meet an old salt at Whitstable who has not at one time or another served on the Favourite. "Ah," they murmur when she is mentioned, and sigh for a youth long past.'[2]

There was an urgency in the situation for a new concrete wall was being constructed along Island Wall and, approaching from either side, was rapidly closing the gap through which the boat must pass. So for £50 the Favourite was purchased. There remained just the task of moving her some forty yards up the steeply inclined beach to a 'safe haven' on a vacant plot besides Mr Janes' cottage. To effect this 'last voyage' he had gathered the talents of an ex-naval officer, the brawn of six able-bodied seamen - a winch, railway sleepers, and several pounds of grease - and a good supply of pink gin and mild ale, to be accompanied by sausages and fresh-baked rolls. Something of a party atmosphere was envisaged as, presumably, the Favourite would slowly climb to her resting place.

'A sizeable crowd had collected, among them a number of salty old Jonahs who shook their heads sorrowfully, muttering that this wasn't the way to go about it. She needed a block and tackle fore and aft, she was probably bolted down, she'd fall to pieces, she needed a slipway, she'd never budge and so on. They constituted a self-appointed jury assembled to bring in nothing but an adverse verdict.'

The sleepers were laid and well greased, the winch, dripping oil, was firmly fixed to its block of concrete and the cables attached to the boat, and the six men divided three to each handle on the winch. 'One, Two, Three - Heave! The cables trembled, six lusty men thirsty for beer struggled for the mastery of those recalcitrant handles. Would they turn, would those well-oiled gears ever engage?'

Alas, no, the Jonahs were proved right. The boat did not budge, it was the winch which gave way. During the time for refreshment and reconsideration which followed there appeared from the onlookers a Mr Dadd. Now he, it appeared, had tractors, and a motor winch, which with those suitably attached - 'well, he would do the job for fifteen quid.' During the following week, however, it bcame clear all was not quite so straightforward - 'It's the tide, you see', explained Mr Dadd. The vehicles had to be on and off the beach at low tide, else they might be marooned and there was work elsewhere the following day.

So a suitable time was agreed for early the next Saturday morning. The two tractors and a lorry were positioned; the cables attached to the winch and all was set. With engines started, slowly with ominous creaking the Favourite began to edge forward. The bow reached the steepest part of the beach, began to climb, when the motor winch packed up. There the boat rested, tipped up like 'a lion rampant'. A further ten pounds and the challenge: Mr Dadd confessed that 'he didn't like to be beat', and a second attempt was arranged for the following Saturday. And at last, with four tractors and what a local shipwright described as 'brute force and ignorance' combined, they triumphed. The Favourite reached her resting place alongside the cottage on Island Wall. 'She'll never feel the swell again,' said one aged fisherman sadly.

But Nature knew otherwise. Some months later on the night of Saturday 31st January 1953, a north east gale which had been blowing all day intensified. The sea was piling up with great waves battering the shore and high tide was yet to come. Many locals feared a storm surge was developing: that special combination of wind and tide which had marked the history of Whitstable with destructive floods. By 2 a.m. the storm had not abated and with high tide far above its normal level huge waves began to crash over at many points along the sea-wall[3].

At Island Wall water swept through gaps between the cottages backing the beach and then poured down into the houses across the road, and on to turn the golf course into an inland lake. It was a night of terror for hundreds of people trapped in many of the low-lying parts of the town. They could do nothing but watch the water flood the ground floor of their homes and creep steadily up the stairs towards the bedrooms where they had taken refuge. As daylight came the town awoke to the extent of the calamity and hundreds of volunteers set to work to rescue the marooned and to relieve their distress. Some 2000 people had been rendered homeless.

And how had the Favourite fared on this night of destruction? The old ship had held fast as the waves dashed over her and the waters swirled past. Had she remained on the beach, then, like other vessels along the shore, she would have been lifted up and hurled inshore, battering cottages, and her frame reduced to splintered wood.

'When the flood subsided and the old sailors saw the Favourite fast on her moorings, they shook their heads mysteriously, whispering that it was a miracle. Maybe it was. But then again she had shown that she will had a will of her own. Perhaps on the awful night she thrilled to feel the waves as they tried to tempt her back to the sea.'[2]

Safe and secure the Favourite now became the focus of the Hurford Janes' garden activities. To provide more headroom inside the hold, which it was planned would be turned into a galley and saloon, a coach roof was carefully constructed on the foredeck. Here family and friends would sunbathe and chat. Among the many visitors were Mr and Mrs Peter Cushing from along the Wall at Wave Crest. A picturesque sight, the old boat was painted and often photographed.

'...officialdom was not slow in discovering her arrival beside Island Wall. "There will be complaints," said the bureaucrats (there were none of course). "What are you going to do with her?" they asked, a meaningful glint in their eyes. "Restore her so that she is seaworthy for an unspecified voyage in the indefinite future," was Mr Janes' reply. "Ah, but what about the rates?" - and "Favourite" was immediately surrounded by little fat men crawling on their hands and knees attempting to measure the length of the keel. There was nothing in the by-laws about the rateable value of old oyster smacks, and thus, after a flurry of activity, nothing more was heard.'

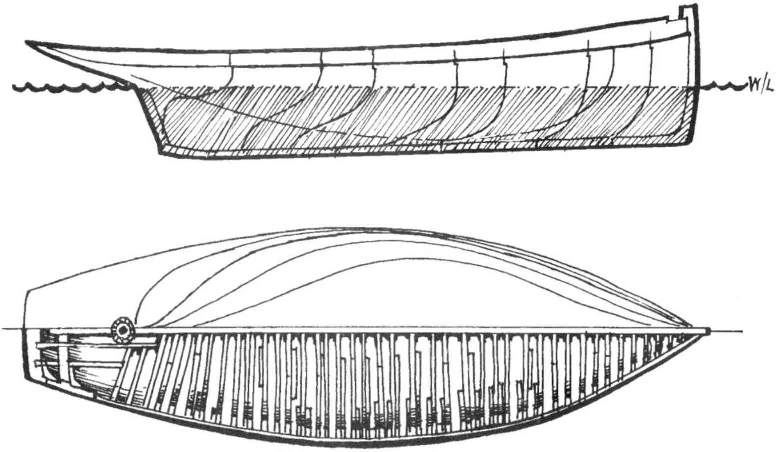

Profile and plan view of the Favourite's 'Lines'

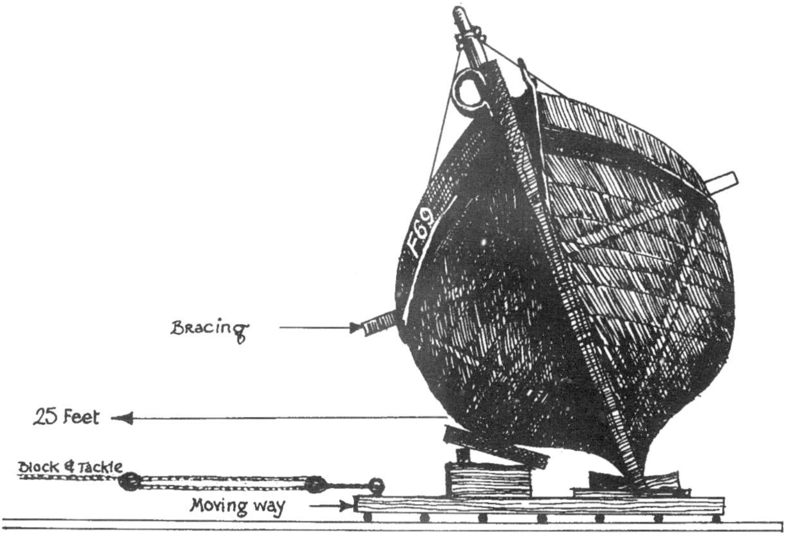

Diagram to show how the old 'Favourite' was moved to a new site.

The years passed and in 1970 her rescuer Harry Hurford Janes decided he must sell his cottage and the old ship lying beside. There were promises that the Favourite would be looked after, but deterioration began to set in - her timbers drying, her seams began to open up, vandals removed her fittings and holes began to appear in her sides. Fears grew that this attractive feature of Island Wall, a reminder of Whitstable's great past, would soon face ruin and removal.

In 1977 once again the future of the Favourite was in doubt as the owner of the cottage required the boat to be removed from his garden. Local residents and others interested in local history were determined that this relic of the past should be preserved and so a Trust was formed to acquire ownership and secure the boat on a permanent site[4]. Happily, adjacent to the garden was a narrow plot which, through the City Council and the Oyster Fishery Company, was made available at a peppercorn rent. Now the problem was to manoevre the boat across to the new site; over the years timbers had become rotten and many joints broken. 'You won't do it,' was the advice from the local shipyard.

An enthusiastic team set to work undaunted. Local school pupils levelled the ground; the mast was taken down and two tonnes of concrete removed from the hull; the timbers were braced with joists and steel wire.

The Favourite was to be moved sideways by setting down four slipways of groyne planks. Then the boat was to be gradually raised on to another set of planks resting on rollers made from scaffold tubing.

'Free beer (Whitbread-Fremlins) and copious hot dogs, newspaper coverage and personal invitation produced 50 volunteers for the move. A Safety Officer was appointed first, then some single-minded organization to protect the boat from over enthusiasm. Tom Porter, a retired builder, provided rope pulleys and knowledge to organize 12 hefties into an efficient but gentle machine. Our calculations (and guesses!) proved correct, the boat slid smoothly but at an angle to the ways. Frequent adjustments to the rollers were required and even a small stone stopped work for ten minutes. The 25 foot move took 3 hours.'

So the Favourite, now consisting of the open hull timbers, came to rest for the second time. Immediate work was to place concrete supports beneath the keel and fit internal tie-rods; the hull was liberally treated with creosote to preserve the woodwork.

The Trust has continued its endeavours: laying out and fencing the site; an information board has been erected and preservation work has to continue.

Alas, the passage of time and neglect has left but the shell of the vessel which was launched at the yard of John Dyason in 1890. Registered at Faversham, F69, the Favourite was typical of the fishing smacks used on the oyster grounds. Carvel built, that is the planks fitted flush together, she was not a large boat: her dimensions being 13.7 metres in length overall, 11.5 metres at the waterline and 4.06 beam. The draught was 1.4 metres aft and 1.09 forward. Essentially therefore a long and shallow boat with the distinguishing Whitstable feature of a 2.4 metre long shallow counter at the stern, probably designed to increase the working space for dredging. The Favourite had a sloping keel turning up towards the rudder, enabling the helmsman to turn the boat into deeper water the moment the keel should touch bottom, an unusual feature. This was a manoeuvrable boat: the lines showing a smooth, fair, fast haul which may reflect the influence of contemporary yacht design. The Favourite, like many other smacks, raced in local regattas. The low freeboard would have given little protection from the elements; although used mainly in coastal waters, rough weather could certainly be encountered. She had the typical cutter rig of mainsail, topsail, foresail and jib[5].

At Whitstable such a craft was called a yawl. This ancient word is of course of Norse origin and appears in Scandinavia as 'yol' and in the

Orkney and Shetlands as a 'yole'; it originally described a small open boat. The word has now become used for a specific type of rig: cutter style as on the Whitstable smacks but with the addition of a small mizzen mast on the stern[6].

The 'bird's eye' map of Whitstable drawn by Jared Hill of Canterbury in 1725 (p. 44) shows four vessels off-shore, all of the bawley type[7]. These small boats, with their straight cut sterns and boomless, loose-footed mainsail, continued to be widely used along the Thames estuary, especially for shrimping. Presumably as the oyster fishery grew in the second half of the eighteenth century - there were 22 boats employed in 1734 and by the 1790s almost 70[8] - larger, more purpose-built craft appeared as the working of the oyster beds became more extensive. These smack were clinker-built craft, that is with overlapping boards, 25 to 30 feet in length usually with pole-masted cutter rig, though some had a long topmast on which a jib-headed or gaff topsail was set[9].

By mid-century the smacks or yawls had become even larger and were now carvel built, with massive frames and deadwood to provide extra strength for the frequent grounding which occurred on the shore. The clinker-built vessels continued in use but had to have their timbers doubled or even occasionally trebled to extend their life when the constant grounding and rising with the tide caused too many leaks. The carvel built craft developed the counter sterns, and topmasts to provide more light weather sail area[10]. Many of these developments are attributed locally to Jonathan Morday, a Foreman of the Oyster Company in 1850[11].

The Favourite, as has been described, was built in the style of these later smacks for Edward Carden, the landlord of the beer-house, the Fisherman's Arms, which was no. 36 Island Wall. This probably did a very local trade for nearby cottages and shipyards; close by was the Kings Head, well-known as a centre for the divers, and almost opposite was the Guinea Inn[12].

Edward Carden

Belonging to a Whitstable sea-faring family Edward was born at Whitstable in 1840. In 1862 he joined the Metropolitan Police and then six years later he was forced to retire having suffered injury to a leg in apprehending a burglar. He had attained the rank of Inspector. Coming back to Whitstable he set himself up as a supplier of maritime goods at 30 Island Wall; this is later described as a twine-store. He probably took over the lease of the Fishermen's Arms in the late 1880s. In Whitstable fashion he was given a nickname: 'Pikey'.

'Mr Carden gained a reputation in the town for the enthralling accounts he gave of his police force experiences. The police uniform worn at the time of his service consisted of a swallow-tailed coat and top hat, whilst rattles were carried instead of whistles. Despite their resplendent dress, however, the police officers were not generally regarded with any degree of affection, and vigilance was always necessary if 'accidents' and similar happenings were to be avoided'.[13]

In 1906 the Fishermen's Arms was closed by the owners, Faversham brewers Shepherd Neame, under the Government scheme to reduce the number of licensed premises in the country. Mr Carden remained there and purchased the property in 1912, continuing until his death at the age of ninety in 1930

To what extent Edward Carden himself sailed is uncertain. The Favourite had as its first Master Charles Camburn, who lived in a cottage at 30 Island Wall. But Edward himself is also listed as Master of the Gilpin, a boat owned by relatives William and Henry Carden. The Favourite would mainly have been engaged in the oyster fishery and it may also have assisted in salvage work with another member of the Carden family. There is certainly a strong tradition of a little involvement with the 'free trade' of smuggling in brandy and tobacco which certainly continued on a local scale. Within the family the story is told of a sudden and unexpected visit of the Excise men to the Fishermen's Arms, too quick for a barrel of illicit brandy to be secreted away. Quick-thinking Mrs Carden promptly sat down on the barrel, arranged her long skirts to conceal it from view, and to ensure she was not asked to move during the search, commenced to suckle her young baby.

The oyster smack, the yawl, was designed to facilitate the process of dredging, by which the oysters were lifted from their bed. The dredge consisted of a triangular iron framework supporting the bag or 'ground' with a 'rigging' made up of interlocking metal rings rather like chain mail. The

lower part of the frame was flattened and angled so that the bag would scrape across the sea bed without tearing it up. The dredges were usually operated as a fleet of five or six, working in pairs with the odd one at the stern. To avoid fouling, the dredges varied in weight and length of rope or 'warp': at the bow the heaviest with the shortest warp and at the stern the lightest with the longest warp. Normally the dredges ranged in weight from 20 lbs to 28, though much heavier ones were used for deep-sea work. There was usually a crew of four with the skipper managing the stern and also steering[14].

Dredging the oyster grounds was carried out on the ebb tide, not towing as when trawling for fish, but gently tacking broadside on to the tide. If the wind was with the tide, the main and jib sheets were slackened right off and the foresail hard to windward; if against the tide then more sail was required: the main and jib sheets kept fairly tight and the foresail to windward.

After the dredge was 'shot' over the side and run out the required length, the warp was hitched to the rail by a breakable 'stopper' so that if it caught on an obstruction this would give way, allowing the remainder of the rope to run out with a small buoy at the end, so floating until recovery. In this way loss of gear was minimised.

The dredge was pulled up over the side of the boat and its contents tipped out of the 'ground' by grasping the 'catch-stick' at the base. The dredge was then 'shot' again and the heap on the deck sorted or 'culled'. Marketable oysters, usually those of four years or older, were chipped off the 'cultch' to which they clung (usually pebbles or shell) with a sharp knife, the 'cultick'. The 'cultch' and the immature oysters, the 'gash', was then 'shaded out', that is pushed back into the sea through the ports in the bulwarks. Vermin such as starfish and crabs, and harmful smothering weed were piled up on one side of the boat, hopefully much of it to be sold to farmers as manure. The oysters were packed in tubs or boxes, or simply collected in nets, to be brought ashore in the 'skiff', the small rowing boat which the smack had towed. Smacksmen from other places would recognise a Whitstable craft not only by certain subtleties of line and rig, but especially by the 'skiff' being towed on a long painter attached to a ringbolt in the stern, and by the removeable dredging ports in the bulwarks; the smarter vessels having them secured in place by lanyards when not in use.

The famous Whitstable oyster ground, the 'Shoal', stretched along the coast for two miles to the east of the long shingle ridge, The Street, extending seaward for about one and three quarter miles. The total area was about six square miles but the actual laying ground of about a mile square was on the northern side, the landward section being used as an anchorage. The dredgermen had more in common with farmers than other fishermen for the successful production of oysters on a large scale required systematic and careful cultivation; as many as 40 million lay on the beds in various stages of growth in the mid-Victorian heyday. Oysters grew best under special conditions: relatively shallow and sheltered water with plenty of clean cultch, but never completely uncovered so that they were protected from frosts, and especially off a coast where streams of fresh water brought down food in the form of microscopic vegetable material.

The dredgermen tended and cared for their beds: they were demarcated with beacons and guarded with three 'watch boats' against poachers; weeds and vermin were removed, cleaned shells were laid as additional cultch, and the oysters were moved several times during growth to end on the best fattening section of the ground. The great uncertainty was the renewal of the bed on the release of hundreds of millions of minute oyster larvae in the breeding season, called the 'fall of spat'. Many factors could determine whether this was prolific or meagre. Hence it was often necessary, at very considerable expense, to collect more spat or baby oysters - 'brood' at one year and 'half-ware', two years old - from other beds to maintain productivity.

Working the Whitstable oyster ground had continued down the centuries as the prerogative of the Freeman: the eldest son being admitted at 16, others at the age of 21 having served a seven year apprenticeship. Only in 1896 did a growing financial crisis cause the traditional system to end; being replaced by a modern share-holding Company with boats being hired as required. There had, however, always been general smacks working out on the common 'flats' extending over an area of some 30 square miles beyond the regulated beds of the local grounds. These were the Faversham and Seasalter grounds with ancient rights, like Whitstable, stretching back to the Middle Ages, and the Ham ground established further out in the Swale estuary in 1865 and amalgamated with Seaslater in 1893. Edward Carden was not a Freeman so the Favourite would have operated on the 'flats'.

Out on the common grounds there were oyster beds as Skipper Albert Stroud recalled: *'When working on the Kentish Flats we used 'marks' on the land to help us whenever we found a patch of ground that was more profitable to work than the general run, and this was where a good fisherman scored, for so many of them never bothered about taking 'marks' from prominent objects ashore. The same thing applied to the nature of the sea-bed. This varied a lot, and if you took notice of your position in clear weather, and the sort of material you were dredging up, in foggy weather a good fisherman would know just where he was by heaving a dredge overboard and noting its contents when hauled up.*

'When dredging for oyster you had to go with the tide... Two dredges would keep you working as hard as you could go, heaving, hauling, culling-out the oysters from the rubbish and hauling again as soon as this residue was 'shaded' overboard. This would go on without a break for the whole of the ebb... By the time you had finished you were just about finished too, having had a gruelling and back-aching few hours without let-up. Bad enough and hard enough when there was plenty to be caught, for that did take some of the sting out of it, but in the latter years, when oysters got very scarce, it was heart-breaking as well'.[14]

Whenever possible the oyster companies relied on the spat originating from their own beds, but since it floated on the tide or was drifted by the wind, it was often deposited all along the 'flats' where the fishermen would gather it and also later lift the 'brood', the tiny baby oysters to sell for restocking, as 'Sonny' Stroud described:

'When I first went on the water there was a terrific lot of spat here... it went down with the tide and fell off down Herne Bay. There was so much there they called it 'The Confetti Bed'. You had to go down there and you caught everything to do with oysters - brood, small or large. Every one was 5s. a wash. That was just over five gallons, five and a quarter gallons. You fancy, a shilling a gallon, and most of the oysters was only as big as shillings themselves!... We sold ours to the Seasalter and Ham Company and they used to have a foreman down there. Now this here was a measure used to be a little tup and of course, if you had a wash measure of water it would be level wouldn't it? Well, with oysters it wasn't. It had to have a round top! He used to say, "A few more on" and you used to have to put a few more on.'[15]

When the local spat proved insufficient it would be brought across from Essex where the protected waters of the long narrow estuaries prevented the dispersal much more effectively. Certainly the Favourite engaged in this trade. Larger smacks went much further afield to obtain brood and half-ware: round to Falmouth and Ireland, and along the coasts off Jersey, France and Portugal. These oysters, however, could not be sold later as the prized 'natives': they could be distinguished by the colour of their shells.

After the Whitstable ground was commercialised in 1896 the company only retained a small number of boats on a permanent basis, hiring additional ones as required. 'Sonny' Stroud described the system of working:

'There always used to be a foreman on the oyster beds... His job, mostly, was to tell you what you had to do when you got out there and what time you all had to start work. You might have to turn out any time, say three o'clock in the morning, and you worked six hours on the grounds. There wasn't much water on the beds, only about two fathoms and a half, and they were all cut up into squares. They'd have poles all over them. One might have a painted piece of canvass on it. Another might have two. Or it might just be a square or there might be a hole cut in the middle.

'One of these squares might just have brood on it, little bits of oysters; then they'd have three or four all fit to sell next year. It was all organised... You had to go and work where you got your orders. They might turn round and say "Go up on number four ground and catch ten bags", twenty bags,

whatever it was. We used to work six hours on the ground then but we had to sail out there in our own time... (then) the foreman would put a flag up or a bag on a pole and then there'd be a proper race to get home.'[16]

In the years just prior to the First World War, although there had been a decline in the oyster industry - rising prices now made the oyster a delicacy rather than a common food - there was still a fleet of around 90 smacks at Whitstable. Following the war years trade slowly revived as the neglected beds were brought back into cultivation and restocked, increasingly with the hardier Portuguese and the 'rock' oysters. For the flatsmen therefore there was usually work on the grounds and they would also engage in general fishing for herring, sole, or plaice, or in the season go shrimping or spratting, raking for cockles or dredging for whelks. During the oyster closed season from May to August the men often sought employment crewing the large racing yachts - popular at the time, working on cruise liners, or offering boat trips to holiday makers.

During the spring of 1921 the first of a series of disasters hit the Whitstable beds which ultimately almost ended the industry. Shells were dredged closed but empty and by the following year it was estimated that three quarters of the stock on the beds had been destroyed and the local 'native' almost wiped out. Eventually the cause was traced to a parasite *Hexamita* which had probably been introduced with oysters from America. Considerable unemployment resulted among the fishermen and many emigrated with their familes, especially to Canada. Perhaps it was this situation - or was it age at 82 - which caused Edward Carden to sell the Favourite to the Oyster Fishery Company in 1922?

The beds were gradually restocked, mainly with oysters from Brittany and Portugal, but the struggling companies were hit hard again by losses in the exceptionally cold winter of 1929. Demand, too, had declined: restaurants served the easier and contemporary prawn cocktail instead of oysters.

During many of these later years with the Oyster Company the Favourite's master was a member of another of Whitstable's maritime families: Alfred 'Dido" Foreman; a man born on Island Wall. In 1931 he was joined by his son Arthur who had started work in the Oyster stores at the age of 13. He later described those days: He was paid 25 shillings a week. As he grew more experienced he packed the better grades of oysters and eventually went on to culling or sorting. As he said:

'In order to get a man's wages you had to go out on the boats in the closed

season during the summer and transfer the mature oysters from the nursery to other pieces of ground. They would then be easier to get at in the winter.'

Then, remembering his time on the Favourite:

'The dredgers brought 300 bushels of oysters ashore each day. When the tide was right off, Bob Nutten, the carrer, would bring his cart on to the beach and take them up to the stores. After being packed they were taken to Whitstable station amd sent up on the train to London'.

He continued working on the Favourite until the Second World War blew the bottom out of the oyster trade. 'All the wealthy Londoners who used to buy the oysters left the city during the evacuation,' he said.

The smacks were beached, Arthur's father went to work at Whitstable gasworks and Arthur himself did war work for boatbuilders Anderson, Rigden and Perkins.

When the Germans attempted to bomb Whitstable harbour some of the smacks, including the Favourite, were damaged and Arthur helped pull them up on to a piece of ground besides Anderson's boatyard in Island Wall.'[17]

And there for some years the old boat remained.

'From time to time her owner - and others with less title - removed parts of her gear or rigging and she took on the appearance of a wreck. Children played pirates on her deck. They cut the ropes securing the shrouds to the chain-plates and swung from the mainmast like the Commandos they had seen on films. At dusk, lovers made her their trysting place and many a lad stole his first kiss in the shadow of her hull. Sometimes a local washer-woman strung a clothes line from her bow, dressing the ship overall.'[18]

And then in due time there came to the rescue, as we have seen, Henry Hurford Janes...

References

1. Faversham News 29.7.1977, 'Will Favourite win race against time?, article by Ralph Bayliss Mills.
2. **Janes**, Henry Hurford, '**Ship Ahoy**', article in Sebrof News (House Journal of Price, Forbes & Co Ltd) pp.38-40.
3. For a fuller account of **storm surges** and the effects of the **1953 flood** at Seasalter see Chapter 3 and references.
4. Banbury PJ, 'Whitstable **Oyster Yawl Favourite** 1890-1980', Bygone Kent v.1 No.2.
5. Banbury PJ, ref. 4 above; information from the Register of Shipping and information published by the Favourite Trust.
6. Coombe, Derek, '**Fishermen from the Kentish Shore**', Meresborough Books 1989, chapter 7 'Whitstable', especially p.105.

The 'Favourite' as she is today.

7. Manuscript sketch-map '**Seasalter Fishery** as claimed by Sgt Knott' 1725 by Jared Hill. Canterbury Cathedral Library, BB Seasalter No 5. Copy at Whitstable Museum Archive.
8. **Hasted** E 'The History and Topographical Survey of the County of Kent' 2nd ed. in 12 vols. 1797-1800, reprinted EP Publishing Ltd 1972, v. VIII, chapter 'The Hundred of Whitstaple' v. VIII p.507.
9. March EJ, '**Inshore Craft of Britain**: In the Days of Sail and Oar', v.2 Ch. 1 'Kent Coast' especially pp.16-23.
10. Coombe, Derek, ref. 6 above, p.105.
11. Research papers of Capt. R Young of Whitstable, held by the author.
12. **Edward Carden**, his career and family: information from the researches of family descendants.
    For the '**Fishermen's Arms**' see Pike G, Page M, Cann J, 'Ales and Tales - Pubs in the Story of Whitstable', Whitstable Improvement Trust 1993 p.51.
13. WT 6.12.1930, obituary notice for Mr Edward Carden.
14. Sources for the Oyster Industry:
    a) Collard AO, 'The **Oysters and Dredgers of Whitstable**' Joseph Collard London 1902, especially pp.74-78.
    b) Pike G, Cann J, Lambert R, '**Oysters and Dredgermen**', Compass Publications Whitstable 1992, especially pp.16-21.
    c) Stroud, Skipper Albert, '**The Half-penny Oyster**' East Coast Digest, June 1976 p.16.
    d) Winstanley M, 'Life in Kent at the Turn of the Century' chapter 8 '**Whitstable and its Oyster Dredgers**' p.107.
15. Described by 'Sonny' Stroud in ref. 14 (c) above p.111.
16. 'Sonny' Stroud as above, p.113.
17. WT 1979 '**Memories of oysters and the 15-hour days**', article interviewing Arthur Foremen, 21.12.1979.
18. Janes HH, ref. 2 above, p.38.

10 THE WINDMILL ON BORSTAL HILL

'No windmill can have been more majestically situated; though its sails would never turn again it lived on to serve as a charted landmark that gave the local seamen bearings on their fishing ground. To the north of Whitstable Borstal Hill rose steeply from sea level to a height of some 200 feet, its shoulders sloping gently to the east and west. It commanded a superb view of the approaches to London River. On a clear day the coast of Essex, the opposite shore of the estuary, could be seen and lost to sight in mid-horizon. To the westward lay the Isle of Sheppey, separated from the marshes of the mainland by the broad reaches of the River Swale flowing eastward to mingle its muddy water with the sea-salted Thames in Whitstable bay. Over this delta landscape the sun set in splendour through the industrial haze of London.

'The windmill stood just below the crest of Borstal Hill, its octagonal base dug into the clay slope like the butt of a rifle into a marksman's shoulder. The brick base, its wall about two feet thick, was divided into two floors, a semi-basement and a first floor bare of machinery and 24 feet overall. On this foundation stood the wooden mill, its four floors tapering gradually until the topmost was about 12 feet in diameter, ringed by a circular geared traverse on which the cap and the great sweeps would be brought head to wind and held there by sturdy locking gear.'

Such was the memory of artist and writer Laurence Irving looking back over some sixty years in his book 'The Precious Crust' to his boyhood encounter with the mill which stands high on the brow of Borstal Hill overlooking the town of Whitstable[1]. His parents were well-known stars of the Edwardian stage: his father HB Irving was the younger son of the famous Victorian actor Sir Henry Irving; his mother was a 'darling' of the stage, Dorothea Baird. They had first come to Whitstable to visit Frank Tyars, a

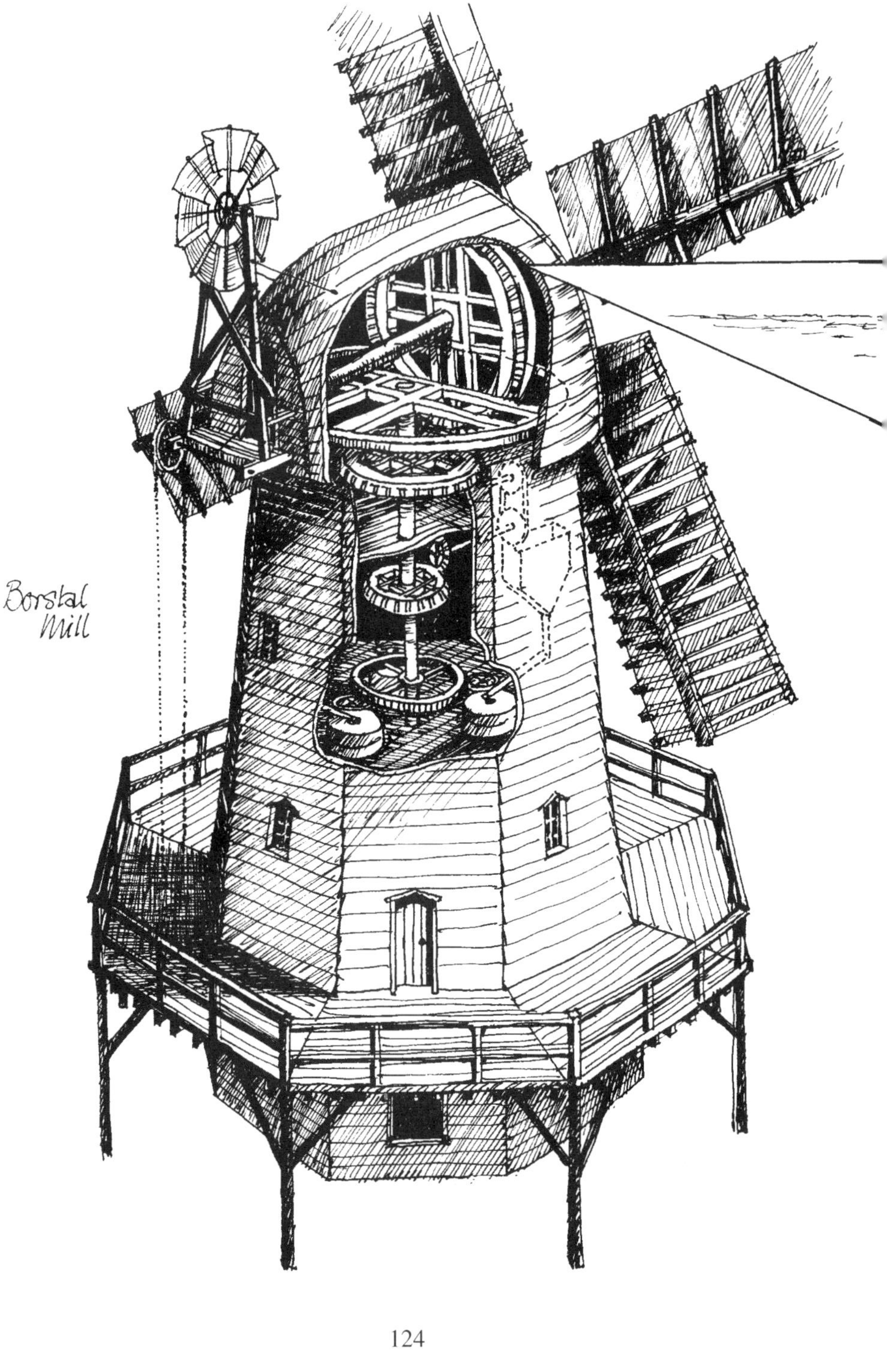
Borstal
Mill

Lawrence Irving as a child, playing in the mill.

former member of the Lyceum Theatre Company, Sir Henry's great band of players. In the early 1890s he had purchased an old farmhouse 'Grimgill' at the foot of Borstal Hill. As Laurence Irving recalled, 'For many years past prudent actors had, like sea captains, preferred to put their savings into real estate, thereby ensuring lodging and livelihood in their retirement'. As we shall see later quite a few personalities of stage and screen have also found Whitstable an attractive and quiet retreat from the bustling metropolis.

Thus when the mill property came up for sale Mrs Irving was easily persuaded by Frank Tyars to buy it, attracted by its panoramic views over town and bay. The miller's cottage was converted into a weekend retreat suitable for family and entertaining friends and in the three acres of ground Dorothea could indulge her passion for gardening. The disused black smock-mill, now a little forlorn without its sails, they left 'as a picturesque feature of their property but had no desire to meddle with it or to make use of it.'

For the young boy Laurence, aged nine in 1906, living in a world dominated by theatrical personalities, the windmill offered an escape into a private world all his own: 'That summer I entered into my domain - a tower, not of ivory but of many kinds of wood butted, scarfed, bolted and treenailed together in perfect symmetry soaring skywards.'

'To a curious boy each floor had its own enchantment. The first provided a spacious battlefield for the waging of the Little Wars in which HG Well's fertile imagination had recently deployed millions of tin soldiers on thousands of nursery floors with his precise tactical manoevres and assessment of havoc wrought by toy artillery.

'The second floor was crammed with rough-hewn machinery - wheels geared with apple-wood cogs, grading drums driven by leather belting, and stone governors hanging from the ceiling like giant bats. Though these mechanisms were, as it were, petrified and would rattle and rotate no more, in their suspended animation they made a cave of stalactic wonders. On this floor large doors opened onto a wooden gallery that ran round the mill. The miller aloft, like the master-mariner on the poop deck, always had his eye cocked on the weather. Caught napping by a black squall he might lose his sails or worse. So he constantly conned the sky for signs of any shift of wind, scanning its cloud patterns, ready at the drop of his white hat to clatter down the ladders and from this gallery to open his shuttered canvas to spill the force of a gale or to swing the cap head to wind. There, on windy days with the spreading sweeps above me, I would imagine myself on the flying bridge of a great ship.

'The third floor was covered with three pairs of boxed-in grinding stones each with an iron shaft thrusting upwards through the ceiling to engage the driving wheels on the top floor. The intermediate floor was divided into bins, little cells with strangely angled wooden walls in which I could crouch in some discomfort but in unassailable privacy with a book or drawing pad.

'But my most daring delight was to climb up into the cap, to straddle the fat windshaft and, clambering through the spreading spokes of the great driving wheel, to work my way to the square trap door that opened onto the huge iron axle into which the intersecting sweeps were wedged. Unbolting it and and lifting it to one side with difficulty for, like everything in the windmill, it was solidly constructed, I could gaze from my Olympian perch over the vast panorama framed in the massive butts of the sweeps. The cap had been anchored for the last time to face north-west, the quarter from which the mill would have to face the fiercest buffetings of the wind (for the brow of the hill behind it broke the force of the south-westerlies). Sitting on the

frame of the trap door, my legs dangling in space, I hardly dared look down upon the garden vertically below. But, searching the skyline, I could sometimes see the silver thread of the Medway to the west and to the north the mainland behind the Essex coast, and the whole sweep of the estuary, dotted with ships steaming and tacking on their occasions. Best of all was to sit astride the windshaft where it entered the cap in a gale of wind that set the sweeps thrumming in their sockets, so that I seemed to be straddling a living monster that I could feel to be alive and trembling between my thighs.'

Here, then, in the old abandoned windmill the young boy had found not only a playground and a private world to be filled by his imagination, but also a deeper feeling which was to be a guiding force throughout his life; 'surrounded by such an assembly of skills and materials I came above all things to desire to make and to do, to prefer practice to theory.'

As may happen with the child of the professional couple absent for long periods from home, and with the gaps later of boarding school, there grew up between Laurence and his parents a degree of reserve in their relationship and for him 'a resistant self-sufficiency'. Yet 'Dolly', his mother, was, as he acknowledged, a warm-hearted and generous person, who took a great interest in a London charity for children from deprived homes. In the summer when free from theatrical commitments it was her delight to fill her garden at the Mill for the day with visitors from the dismal backstreets of the city. So whilst her son day-dreamed alone in his tower of wonder, down below the scene was of bustle and laughter.

After the death of 'HB' in 1919 Mrs Irving continued to live at the Mill. Here many personalities from the world of the stage and now, of course, the screen, would travel down for weekend parties: amongst them such great artists as Constance Collier and Ellen Terry, Douglas Fairbanks and Charlie Chaplin. A frequent visitor, too, was Lady Irving, widow of the great actor, who was especially fond of the young Laurence. She had lost both her sons, for HB's elder brother had been drowned with his wife when the liner 'Empress of Ireland' had been sunk by a U-boat on its voyage to America in 1914.

In due course Laurence himself became owner of the Mill and with his affection for the place he decided to build a large house to accommodate his family, attaching it to the mill itself[2]. He was now well established as a designer for the stage and cinema and so the first floor of the mill was converted into a studio with a lithographic press below on the ground floor. So

The Irvings Mill House

it was, as he wrote in his book 'The Precarious Crust', the windmill became 'successively my refuge, my gymnasium and finally my workshop to which, in due course my home became an annex.'

In addition to the new building the old windmill also received attention. All the weatherboarding and staging was replaced taking the greatest care to preserve the original character; for this restoration work he received a Certificate from the Society for the Protection of Ancient Buildings - a certificate which he himself had earlier designed. After moving into the house in 1927 Laurence set off in a boat to cruise through the waterways of Holland, that land of windmills; a voyage which he recounted and illustrated in his book 'Windmills and Waterways'.

In 1925 Laurence Irving undertook his first theatre commission, beginning a long and highly successful career: in the next 40 years he was involved in 50 major film and stage productions. For Douglas Fairbanks Sr.

he designed the sets for the last silent classic, 'The Man in the Iron Mask' and then 'The Taming of the Shrew' starring Mary Pickford; later came such notable films as Shaw's 'Pygmalion' and 'Major Barbara', and '77 Park Lane'. On the stage amongst many achievements were productions of 'Hamlet', 'the Good Companions' and 'The Nelson Touch'.

With the onset of war in 1939 the Irvings left the Mill and Laurence rejoined the air force; he had trained as a fighter pilot in the last years of World War One. Serving with distinction he was awarded the OBE (Military). Meantime at Whitstable the staging of the windmill provided a splendid observation post for the military to survey a wide stretch of the Thames estuary, and to scan the skies for approaching enemy aircraft.

This break in the occupation of the Mill is a suitable point to look backwards to earlier days and to recount what is known of its history.

It was built in the 1790s probably by one of the Foord family who were great landowners in the area. A sale advertisement of 1808 describes a 'newly erected smock Corn Mill being in Borstal Hill occupied by Joseph Daniels'. The site is ideal for a mill, catching the winds sweeping in across the bay and the downdraft over the brow of the hill also; a predecessor seems to be shown on a Kent map of 1736. In 1851 Wynn Ellis, Lord of the Manor and an extensive landowner (see Chapter Eight) purchased the property from Jane Austin of Upper Hardres for £825. After Daniels the millers are listed as Edward Lawrence and Henry Somerford. A mill like this would be run by two men, and perhaps it was quite common for brothers to take on the work together; here, after Jonathan Rye, came the Callingham brothers and then George and William Dawkins. The mill was originally white, for it was used as seamark by Trinity House. In 1885 when much of the weatherboarding was repaired it was tarred instead of being painted; presumably by this time these old navigational aids were of less significance to local mariners. So, too, the need for the corn mill disappeared and the great sails ceased to work in 1899. The cottage then became a rest-home for retired seamen of the Stanhope Shipping Company from whom the property was purchased by Mrs Irving.

After the war, resuming his career in films and theatre, Laurence Irving now turned his attention to writing: first chronicling the careers and personalities of the Irving family, and then producing two volumes of autobiography. He also developed his skills in line and design with illustrations for a number of books, several with strong affinities with the sea: 'Hakluyt's

Voyages', 'Bligh's Journal of the Voyage of the Bounty' and Conrad's 'Mirror of the Sea'[3].

Throughout all these years whenever possible he also expressed his love of the sea practically in the art of sailing, and in his many paintings in which he so often captured scenes in and around the coastline at Whitstable - the harbour and boatyards, the estuary and the River Swale. Especially in his early work he recorded incidents and scenes which now stand as a record of times gone by.

The Mill continued to be used by the Irving family until 1961. It was then purchased by Mr Harborne who developed the site as the Windmill Hotel, building a line of motel rooms along the entrance driveway. Within the mill the hotel entrance and lounge were created in the base and above was the dining room and bar; around the latter some of the wooden machinery was retained as a feature. Mr Harborne underook major renovation work in 1969 but the projected restoration of the sails to the rather gaunt stocks was not realised. The hotel use was continued by the Ferrari family who purchased the Mill in 1973, making further improvements to the accommodation and developing the ground floor into an octagonal restaurant. Closure came in 1987. Restoration work was again undertaken two years later; the stocks were replaced and fantail and fan added to the cap, but it remained too costly to complete the original appearance by adding the sails. Recently the whole site has been redeveloped with houses replacing the old motel rooms along a road which now leads to a courtyard fronting the mill and its house.

As the town of Whitstable has spread up and along Borstal Hill the original striking position of the Black Mill so well described by Laurence Irving has been lost, but still the upper part of its towering structure catches the eye, just as it did to Turner when he drew his panoramic view towards the harbour from Seasalter which was published in 1826[4].

The Irvings came to Whitstable, as we have seen earlier, through the connection with Frank Tyars who had made his home in the old farmhouse at the foot of Borstal Hill from the early 1890s. There is certainly a tradition that Sir Henry Irving visited him there, but there is no doubt that Frank Tyars influenced others to settle in Whitstable and so began an association between actors and the town which has continued to the present day.

Tyars himself built several houses along Gordon Road which ran alongside his property, and these he sold to fellow thespians of the Lyceum Company, notably Charles Dodsworth and Frances Davis. This connection probably accounts also for the leasing of the 'Towers' at Tankerton for six months in 1895 by the then celebrated dramatist Arthur Wing Pinero. It must have been when visiting Tyars that he and his wife took pity on the livestock driven up and down Borstal Hill and so had a drinking trough placed beside the old tollgate cottage which was almost opposite the farm-house. A replacement still remains today (see illustration p. 75).

Memories of the great days of the late Victorian and Edwardian theatre long survived just down the road from the mill: 'The snuggest, cosiest haven in which a seafaring man ever raised a pewter tankard to his thirsty lips is the bar parlour at the sign of the Two Brewers at Whitstable where the duties of 'mine host' are shared by two brothers whose names are known and honoured in every greenroom in Britain.'[5]

Arthur Bertram, who had been actor-manager to the Irvings, retired to the pub in 1923, and was joined shortly after by his actor brother Frank. These two flamboyant characters delighted in exchanging reminiscences of London theatreland with their customers' yarns of seafaring life. Arthur, who remained landlord until 1956, then well into his eighties, had acquired the set of bells used to great effect in 'The Bells', the story of a man haunted by his conscience when concealing his knowledge of a murder. This was said to the most gripping role performed both by Sir Henry Irving and later by his son 'HB'. These bells Arthur would ring every Sunday morning to announce opening time. So was a link with the London theatre maintained.

From the stage round the Mill one gets a superb view across the old town of Whitstable: to the east the harbour is prominent, and westward one can follow the long stretch of houses runnng along Island Wall facing the sea away towards Seasalter. In contrast to the quiet and charm of today, this was formerly an area filled with the smells, dirt and noise of an industrial area:

'Few strangers trouble to visit Whitstable's island wall, yet it is there, even more than in the High street, that its trade centres. True, the High street can boast numerous and well-appointed shops. But those who would witness the arts of ship-building, boat-building, block and mast-making, sail-making, and a score of operations connected with nautical affairs, should not omit a visit to the island wall. There, too, are the stores of fishermen and dredgermen, and there, on almost any fine day, may be witnessed the unloading of boatloads of the delicious oysters for which the town is famous.' (1882)[6]

After the First World War, with the disappearance of sailing ships, all this maritime activity faded away, with only one shipyard surviving into recent times. Gradually Island Wall began to attract new residents drawn by the quiet and charm of the location: the fishermen's terraces and cottages, the broad expanse of the beach and the wide panorama across the bay towards the Isle of Sheppey; equally attractive when the stormy sea was flecked with foam or on a calm evening with the glorious colours of the setting sun. Initially people bought cottages as weekend retreats and homes for summer holidays, but then succumbed to the place and chose to become permanent residents. And many of these had connections with the theatre and cinema. Dora and Zoe Davis were stars of London revues: they were daughters of Alfred Davis, one-time manager of the Lyceum Theatre[7]. Down where the roadway clings most obviously to the top of the old seawall is the part called Lower Island. Here for many years 'Ye Cottage' was home to Sam, Roger, and Pam Livesey who acted as a focus for many London visitors. Two doors away 'Fagin's Den' hardly disguised the role Albert Ward played in an early film of 'Oliver Twist'[8]. And, of course, for nearly forty years a terrace house overlooking the sea at West Beach, was home to the famous star of stage, film, and television, Peter Cushing[9].

He first came to Whitstable as a visitor, as so many later residents did, bringing Helen Beck, his wife-to-be, to stay with their friend, freelance writer Hurford Janes (a main character in chapter Nine) who had a cottage on Island Wall. After their marriage in 1948, with Peter developing a successful stage career, the Cushings bought a house in London. But both suffered from poor health, Mrs Cushing in particular from a severe bronchial condition. So, as Peter Cushing wrote in his autobiography, their doctor advising 'it was imperative that Helen should breathe as much clean fresh air as possible, we acquired a terrace cottage in the quaint little fishing town of Whitstable, Kent, which we adored.' Initially this was intended to be a weekend retreat, but, 'we were becoming increasingly disenchanted with the changing face of London, and more and more attracted to life by the seaside, where the ozone did Helen so much good, and she appeared to be in better health recently.' So in 1959 their cottage on Island Wall became their permanent home.

In 1960 the Whitstable Times profiled both Peter and Helen Cushing in a series of biographies of important residents; Peter spoke frankly about his early life, which was unusual for him, for he was by nature a very private person.

He described how he grew up in Kenley, then a small Surrey village later to be absorbed into Croydon, and was educated at local schools where he most enjoyed in his older years the painting lessons, rugger, and amateur theatricals - clearly not a scholar. His first involvement with the theatre came about at the age of eleven when, with his brother, he ran a puppet theatre for family and friends. There was no charge for entry, but his brother levied 2d. to get out! The article continued: 'As far back as he can remember he always wanted to go into the theatre and, although his father was a quantity surveyor, he came from a family which had many connections with the theatre. His grandfather had been with Sir Henry Irving and had accompanied him on his tours of Canada and the United States of America. His aunt had acted with Gertie Miller and his step-uncle Wilton Herriot was a well-known actor in his day and had been one of the principals in 'Charley's Aunt'.

As with Laurence Irving, so with Peter Cushing one can see the influence of boyhood interests on the later development of a career. And by chance there is a link again back to the dominant figure of the late Victorian stage, Henry Irving. Peter Cushing did not make the break until he reached the then age of adulthood, 21 years. He recalled how he pestered the manager of the Worthing Repertory with letters seeking a job. When eventually he received an invitation to call from Bill Fraser, the Manager, he thought he had succeeded. Alas, it was really only to tell him to stop being a nuisance. However, when the young man tearfully explained 'I can't go back, I've given up my job', this stirred the Manager's heart and he was given a walk-on part for that very night: a great career was launched.

It was during the war that Peter Cushing and his wife-to-be Helen Beck met, playing the leading roles in Noel Coward's 'Private Lives', Peter being unfit for military service. They were married in 1948 and so began a lifetime of devotion: 'he gives all the credit for his success to his wife, who, he says, has always guided, supported and cared for him magnificently,' quoted the reporter in 1960.

Perhaps because these were early days for the Cushings' life in Whitstable, and for Peter the great fame of his career was yet to come, the reporter was allowed the rare, probably unique, privilege of describing their home on Island Wall, and especially to detail the studio - that sanctum at the top of the house with its views over the sea. Here was a private world where boyish interests and adult hobbies continued away from the professional world.

Peter Cushing at 'Cushing's View.'

'Their house, although it has its fair share of 'ever so house and garden' climbing plants, is a tasteful mixture of old and new and the overall effect is one of order, light and colour. ...at the top of the house on Island Wall he has a Studio - Studio is, perhaps, something of a misnomer, however, for although it has a splendid north window overlooking the bay and one wall is covered with his paintings of Whitstable, the room is by no means just an artist's workshop... It is best described as a den and even a casual glance around it shows the great variety of his interests. Model aeroplanes, which he has made, hang from the ceiling, and in one corner there is a workbench on which there are scores of paper clips, several unfinished models, and an aquarium of tropical fish. In other parts of the room there are bookshelves which chiefly contain children's books, bunks and cabinets, where he houses his collection of model soldiers and cigarette cards. It is altogether a

Peter Cushing in his younger days

delightful room and it expresses his personality as we saw it; not eccentric but splendidly individualistic.'

Peter Cushing said that he loved Whitstable, for although it was flattering to be recognised, people did not intrude. For many years he was a familiar figure riding around on his bicycle and then, after colliding with a dog and breaking his leg, slowly walking by, always ready to exchange a few words as he went to his favourite cafe in Harbour Street. "I've found nothing but kindness and courtesy,' he said, 'I like Whitstable because of its quaintness and charm. It's not pretty but it has character, Dickensian character.'

Appropriately a platform against the sea wall at the beginning of Island Wall was named in his honour 'Cushing's View'. It looks out over the wide open span of the bay which he once described as 'incomparable'. This was where he would paint, watch the birds, and wander over the mud when the tide was out. When Peter Cushing died in 1994 the streets were lined as the cortege passed by, not so much for a man known the world over, but, as the outpouring of letters to the local press revealed, for his gentlemanly courtesy and sincere love of the town and its people[10]. Away from the world of his celebrated career, for nearly forty years Whitstable had been his home.

Laurence Irving and Peter Cushing, having in common long and distinguished careers in the cinema and the theatre, found here in Whitstable a haven away from the pressures of professional life. Like so many others who have visited, returned, and then perhaps resided, both found great pleasure in the old-fashioned charm of the long waterfront with its narrow lane winding along the sea wall, the changing character of the harbour and the jumble of tarred stores and sheds, the neat terraces and the brightly coloured cottages. It still has, as one local put it, 'the tang of the sea', even if the original maritime trades have passed away. Above all, both men loved the sea: that great open expanse of the bay in all itst varying moods, with the views across to Sheppey and the distant shore of Essex and both found great pleasure in seeking to record the special character of this place in watercolour and in paint.

References

1. **Irving, Laurence, 'The Precarious Crust'**, Chatto and Windus 1971 pp.148-49 and 164-67.
2. West J, 'The **Windmills of Kent**', Charles Skilton 1973 pp.77-80, for the history of the mill.
   WT 17.6.61 and 9.5.69, for the later use of the mill.
3. '**Laurence Irving**' - an outline of his career in a biographical note for an exhibition of his work at the Barton Art Gallery, Tenterden 14.6.87.
4. **Turner** JMW, a view drawn for his series 'Ports of England' published as an engraving by J Horsbrugh in 1826. Reproduced as Plate XXXII facing p.243 in Goodsall RH, 'Whitstable, Seasalter and Swalecliffe', Canterbury 1938.
5. WT 4.1.1930.
   Evening Standard 25.4.1946.
6. WT 9.4.1946 quoting from the Whitstable Monthly Gazette, April 1882.
7. WT 1.5.1948 - theatrical background.
8. West D, 'Fourth Portrait of a Seaside Town', Emprint Whitstable 1991 p.8 (note that Pinero did not purchase the Towers as mentioned here. It was rented for six months.)
9. The information for the **career and life of Peter Cushing** is drawn principally from two articles: WT 9.4.60 and Kent Life May 1986, and his book 'Peter Cushing: an Autobiography', Weidenfeld and Nicholson 1986 pp.130 and 136.
10. WT 19.1.1995, 'Souvenir Tribute'.

The Town Museum today

11 THE WHITSTABLE MUSEUM AND GALLERY

Close to the junction between the two parts of Whitstable's busy long main street - the High Street and Oxford Street - one finds the inconspicuous entrance to the town's Museum and Art Gallery. Opened in 1985, it lies tucked away behind the buildings along the street frontage. Beyond the vestibule you come into the large and spacious main exhibition hall, dominated by the bright red of the town's Victorian fire engine and surrounded by displays of artefacts, pictures and photographs illustrating the history of this town. Here is a diver in full gear; there equipment and a film illustrating the famous oyster industry; beyond are scenes of the once busy harbour and models and paintings of the sailing ships which once crossed the seas from Whitstable. The art gallery at the end provides space for lively tempo-

rary exhibitions ranging from the creations of local school children to the work of artists amateur and professional, local and international.

When this building, the old British Legion Hall, was purchased the concerns were for its central location and suitability for conversion into spaces suitable for exhibitions. There was no thought that here was a site and a building which might exemplify much of Whitstable's history, as we shall now find as we explore another of its 'places' and the people' connected with it.

An Inn and a Residence: links with the 18th century

Old property deeds often contain a mine of information for the local historian. From the description of the boundaries, with the names of all the adjacent owners, it is possible to identify the piece of ground and its surroundings. Deeds often contain a recital of the previous owners of the property, often stretching back a century and more. Very often one can then fit this sequence into the wider history of the area.

The deeds for the museum site are a splendid example, for they contain documents giving details from the beginning of the eighteenth century[1]. Then it was a part of a block of land stretching northwards across what is now 1-3 Oxford Street to the ground on which Cromwell Road begins. So we learn that in 1709 there stood here a 'Messuage or Tenement lately called or known by the Name or Sign of the Packett Hoy and formerly of the Three Marriners together with the Barn Stable Garden and Yard thereunto... And also of and in One Piece or Parcel of Pasture Land therewith used and enjoyed Containing by Estimation One Acre and three Roods'.

This inn was then, of course, outside the small village of Whitstable Street, on the busy road linking the landing point at the Horsebridge to the city of Canterbury - a road of sufficient importance to be turnpiked in 1726 as we have seen in Chapter Six. The property had been owned by the Reynolds family since at least the middle of the seventeenth century and was now occupied by Thomas Reynolds. The Packet Hoy Inn seems to have continued for a short time from 1723 as the Canterbury Hoy before closing in 1729.

Traditionally this Thomas Reynolds has been remembered as the leader of a local smuggling gang[2]. In the eighteenth century this illicit trade was rife along the coast of Kent and broadly fell into two categories. Locally there was the small scale smuggling by the fishermen and then there was the highly organised trade when a ship laden with contraband would anchor close in to the shore and the goods would be moved swiftly and efficiently across the country[3]. As was reported in March 1746: 'on the 7th instant a gang of about one hundred and fifty smugglers landed their cargo between Reculver and Birchington and went from the sea coast about 9.0 a.m. Sixty three men and from eighty to ninety horses went by Whitstable and Faversham, and the rest went over Grove Ferry.'[4] To carry out this kind of operation required the outlay of considerable capital, a high degree of organisation and a chain of safe places where the contraband could be secreted en route. The Reynolds family owned or had interests in a series of properties which might well have been used in this way.

Most of the men who were recruited for these gangs were local fishermen and farm workers who welcomed the opportunity to earn money and

gain a small share of the illicit goods. So an inn such as the Packet Hoy could act as a meeting place for the exchange of information on the local revenue men, some of whom were often in league with the smugglers, and to receive instructions when a cargo was due.

Secrecy being part of the operation, knowledge of smuggling can only be gained from local tradition and from newspaper reports of successful actions by the revenue, and these certainly show that towards the end of the eighteenth century Whitstable men were very much involved[5].

A deed of sale of 1779 shows that now there was a property on this site occupied by Redding Pierce, a surgeon,. and previously by John Coltrup, one of the wealthier inhabitants. A glimpse of this Georgian-style residence can be seen in the windows and handsome cornice above the single-storey shop extension to No 3 Oxford Street next to the museum entrance. As a single house this must have been unusually grand for Whitstable; was it perhaps built by Thomas Reynolds out of the profits of the 'free trade'? He died in 1744 at the age of 68.

The Whorlows and the mid-Victorian Town

In 1809 the house and land were sold by descendants of Thomas Reynolds to John Whorlow who as 'Expenditor for the Commissioners of Sewers' had been in charge of the construction of the new sea wall stretching from Reeves Beach to Tankerton. This 'Insett Sea Wall' replaced the original one to the seaward which had been destroyed by the battering of the sea.

The house was now divided into two and in the right-hand part John's eldest son Robert Tritton Whorlow lived, at first working as a boot-and-shoe maker and then from 1825 becoming the town's Postmaster. Later on in life he also acted as Collector of Land Assessed Taxes and Deputy Registrar of Births and Deaths. He died still working at the age of 75 on the last day of December 1876: 'by his invariable courtesy and obliging manner, (he) gained for himself the respect of all his fellow townsmen', recorded the Whitstable Times[6].

He was succeeded by his eldest son, named, in the Victorian tradition, after his father, Robert Tritton Whorlow. He had acted as his father's clerk for many years and had occupied the other half of the house. In February 1879 the Post Office was moved into the main business part of the High Street though times were not good, for Mr Whorlow only received an honoratium of £16-6-8d due to 'the depression in trade and shipping'. He continued as Post Master and then just over a year later the Whitstable Times reported that 'he left home on Tuesday of last week and has not been heard of since'. This disappearance occasioned no further comment, as was the tradition then in this local paper with regard to personal distress, and a replacement was rapidly appointed.

It is now necessary to retrace a few years in order to discover the origin of the building which forms the main hall of today's museum. In 1860

The Whitstable Commercial Academy Circa. 1860 (school)

Robert Tritton Whorlow together with a younger son Albert purchased the house and the adjacent land - the site of which was first described in 1709 - from William Neame on a mortgage of £500 at £6 per cent per annum, and to be redeemed after 7 years. This loan was on the condition that they would 'forthwith erect and build on part of the land or ground hereby granted a Schoolroom 40 feet in frontage or length and 20 feet in depth, the walls thereof to be of good bricks and the roof slated.' This building was tucked in to the rear of the house on one side and a long cottage on the other. Inside, it was just one large schoolroom. To add dignity to the end facing the street there was a crow-stepped gable surmounted by a little bell turret (as in illustration above).

The building of a private schoolroom in a small town like Whitstable was quite unusual and furthermore in 1845, close by, the Whitstable Charities had opened their Trust School which was designed to cater for up to 200 boys. Yet the 'Whitstable Commercial Academy', after it opened in March 1861, was to run for almost twenty years and apparently had up to 100 boys on roll[7]. Clearly the Whorlow's school must have met a demand, doubtless reflecting the growing size and increasing prosperity of the town.

In 1841 the population of Whitstable was around 3,000 and in each of the next three decades it increased by 1000. Over the 30 years from 1841-71 the number of dwellings increased from around 700 to 1100. From the 1840s commerce and industry were flourishing: the fleet in the bay comprised upwards of 70 vessels trading in coastal and foreign waters; ship-building and repairing were therefore spreading along the shore; and the oyster industry was beginning to boom with the insatiable demand of the ever-increasing London market, where oysters were a staple food for the poor[8]. The 'Academy' must have provided a more specialised education for children of tradesmen, master mariners and artisans who could afford to pay more than the 1d. a week which was required at the Trust School.

It was, however, at the Trust School beside St Alphege Church that young Albert Whorlow learnt the art of schoolmastering. When opened in 1845 there was, either side of the accommodation for the Master and the Mistress, a large schoolroom and one classroom for up to 250 boys and 140 girls. Although in reality the numbers on roll were somewhat lower, the only assistance the Master and Mistress had were older pupils from about the age of eleven acting as Monitors, and a few of these moving on to become Pupil Teachers from the age of fourteen. So in 1852 Albert, presumably a pupil since the opening of the school, became one of four Pupil Teachers, and then after five years apprenticeship was appointed an Assistant Teacher at £45 per annum (more funds were available by this time in grants under the Government scheme)[9]. Albert's contract expired in the summer of 1860 and within the year he had his own school. There are no details available, for the 'Academy' never advertised nor was it ever mentioned in the local press; the minutes of the Trust school make no mention of this competing institution. The School closed in 1880 doubtless due to the provision now made by the new 'Board School' which had opened in fine buildings in 1877 (today this is the Whitstable Junior School behind the library).

The Foresters Hall - Whitstable in the 1880s

In March of 1881 the Whorlow's school - the big schoolroom with an additional classroom and office - was purchased by the local branch of the

Ancient Order of Foresters, to provide them with their own premises instead of hiring rooms at the Bear and Key Hotel. The Foresters were one of the largest of the Friendly Societies which had become a major aspect of Victorian life; by this time they totalled some four million members across the country. These benefit organisations had emerged in northern industrial cities during the late eighteenth century as groups meeting together in public houses; convivial gatherings for smoking and drinking from which developed a concern for mutual support through weekly contributions to cope with the financial disasters of sickness and death[10].

The Ancient Order of Foresters Friendly Society

The Foresters were established in 1834, based on a smaller and older society. As with others, it catered for the upper working class and the rapidly expanding lower middle class, reflecting the rising standard of living which enabled men to 'put aside a little each week' against the hazards of 'a rainy day'. The Friendly Societies, therefore, did to some extent embrace men from different class levels and, like the Chapels, helped to bind together Victorian society. Including as they did families with reasonable social and educational standards, the Societies endeavoured to move away from the public house background.

The local court (Prince of Wales No 1902) was established in 1845 and now in 1881 had 341 members with an average age of 33, and they had built up a capital from contributions of £2,816. At the 'Grand Opening' Brother WP Coleman congratulated the members[11]

'...on the affluent circumstances which have enabled them to purchase and beautify the Foresters Hall... Commodious, well ventilated, comfortably seated, curtained and artistically adorned, the Hall is everything that could be desired as a resort for the Order, or for such pleasurable assemblies as that on this occasion. I am sure that you all feel some satisfaction that in our small town there is this outward sign of thrift and independence.'

Mr Coleman continued by outlining the basic concepts on which the Order of Foresters was based:

'Forestry is not an abstraction, but a reality... an association of men united for the highest purposes of philanthropy, viz. the well-being of our

fellow men; to aid and succour the sick and distressed, and to comfort the mourner... There is also a social advantage incidental to our Order. Besides uniting to render less trying the vicissitudes of human existence, we meet for the promotion of social happiness. Associated for purposes alike benevolent and honourable, the frivolity of the profane is never allowed to enter in to our courts.'

In conclusion Brother Coleman emphasised: 'Sober, honest and industrious every member of our Order is expected to be... I urge upon all parents and young men present the importance of incalcating and cultivating habits of thrift.'

However, there were some in Whitstable for whom 'thrift' was an impossible virtue as they existed in dire poverty. A letter to the local paper in March 1880 described 'the distressed inhabitants of Whitstable, numbers of whom have been endeavouring to keep life in their bodies during the winter with a scant meal of mussels often unaccompanied by bread.'[12] During that month the soup kitchen dispensed 600 gallons to the 'deserving poor'. This extreme poverty had been acute that winter due to the severe weather: even the sea had been frozen over well out from the shore, and the casual work on which the labourers relied had not been available.

More widely, however, there was depression beginning to affect Whitstable's two staple industries: shipping and oysters. Ships were getting larger and turning to bigger harbours, and over-exploitation had seriously reduced the return from the oyster beds. A sign of the times was evidenced in the town meeting called by the Vicar, the Revd. HM Maugham, in April 1879 when 'the room was well filled, all classes being represented.'[13]

Acknowledging the decline in trade he advocated turning attention to a rather neglected part of the town's assets: 'make Whitstable more attractive to visitors, either by doing away with those things that might deter visitors from coming here, or by providing them with facilities which may make their stay among us pleasant and agreeable.' There was loud applause then, but little support when the Improvement Trust which was set up asked for donations to implement change. So the beach (the one next to the harbour, for Tankerton was a private estate) was crowded on bank holidays and for Regatta Day, but otherwise with its simple amenities of tea-booths, swings and boat rides, catered mainly for women's and children's groups who wanted a day by the sea without spending more than a shilling.

So the Foresters in their comparative affluence improved their Hall, adding a dignified entrance facing the street proudly engraved FORESTERS HALL (as it remains today). At the rear a kitchen was created to cater for all their social functions, and they also extended the adjacent end cottage as their office. In all they spent £714. Thus the Foresters had a large hall for the meetings of their court and social events: in March 1882, for example, between 70 and 80 sat down to a meal and the party did not break up until 12 o'clock (the Victorians kept late hours: dances frequently went on until four in the morning.)

The Foresters Hall also became an important addition to the amenities of the town, for the only other public hall was at the Assembly Rooms, and this, the old Music Hall, was regarded as a place for entertainments. In July 1881 a Masonic Lodge was formed, apparently reviving an earlier one of 1813. The Lodge took the name 'Graystone' from the Lord of the Manor, the Revd. Arthur Graystone. For the consecration ceremony over 100 brethren gathered from all over Kent. Then in 1882 the 'Jaculars' moved there from the Steam Packet public house: an exclusive group of 21 members, they met for scientific discussion. At their first meeting they engaged in 'the dissection of assorted specimens from the animal and vegetable world' and experimented with 'transverse vibrations of soniferous bodies; (making different sounds by striking different objects!) The Jaculars represented the growing interest in science which was very characteristic of the time.

Also in 1882 there was founded at the Foresters Hall The Whitstable Club by 'some of the principal inhabitants' as the local paper recorded, but it did not indicate their activities. The well-established 'Harmonic Society' moved to the hall for their practices, though they still used the large hall at the Assembly Rooms for their concerts. This sample illustrates the range of social and cultural activities of Whitstable in the 1880s, a town of some five-and-a-half thousand people. The chapels and church were also extremely active within the community, making provision especially for children through the Sunday Schools. Then for labouring men, the representatives of the poorest class, there were the beerhouses: at this time there were over 30 in the central town area, most acting truly as 'the local' for the men in the immediate area seeking company away from small crowded cottages. As in all aspects of social life the licensed premises ranged from the Bear & Key hotel into which a gentleman might go, to the back street beerhouse for the 'rough and ready' men in their working clothes[14].

The Birth of Local Government: 1894

On the last day of December 1894 a group of twelve men met formally in the minor hall of the Foresters: the Urban District Council was holding its first session - town government had arrived[15]. Was this, then, the body which would meet the challenge of the approaching new century in a town in which great distress now prevailed?

Over the preceding months there had been a hard fought campaign. On one side were the die-hard traditionalists who had for at least fifty years opposed any major change or improvement in the town:

'In constituting Whitstable into an Urban District taking in the outlying districts, especially Tankerton Estate, is an immense undertaking, and we had better look well before we leap into the enormous expenditure... (this)... must entail' (John Putwain) .

On the other side were those who strongly favoured more unified control over town affairs, replacing the plethora of authorities and boards which had characterised the growth of Victorian local government:

'Such a body, composed of our own townsmen and sitting in our own town, the general government of the place would work itself out in our midst, and under our immediate criticism.' (William Holden)

The scheme which emerged created an Urban District which included the new estate being laid out at Tankerton, with the boundary swinging around the edge of the existing town, down the west side of Borstal Hill, and ending on the shore to include the houses along Island Wall. Swalecliffe remained separate, so small that it could only have a Parish Meeting. The area from Church Street through the rural area to Seasalter constituted a new Parish Council: Whitstable-cum-Seasalter. Both of these functioned under the larger Blean Rural District Council.

There had been 34 nominations for the UDC of whom 28 eventually stood for twelve places on the new Council. A town meeting in November had made abundantly clear local opinion, passing a resolution stating that they were 'unanimously in favour of supporting candidates pledged to economy.'

What became immediately apparent was that those who already played the significant roles in the town, in business, trades and professions, and in holding offices on the local Boards and in the chapels and the church were the men who formed the body of new councillors. Democracy may have been practised, but the 'old guard' still held sway[16]. Whitstable was a small community of around 6000 people dominated by the marine interests of shipping, ship-building and repairing, and the oyster trade. Furthermore, intermarriage between the often very large Victorian families meant that 'many who held local public office were influenced by the family ties and relationships to which they were subject. Many were closely related, as sons or brothers, others were connected by marriage ties, as cousins, uncles, or by commercial and business interests.'

The influence of this situation on the council was well expressed in a letter to the local paper following the first Council meeting:

...the best intentions of the town are to be sacrificed to personal feelings and private pique. It may be urged that it is early yet to grumble - that the newly formed Board should have a fair start. That is exactly what I had hoped it would have: instead of which a cabal is formed, a majority of the members holding meeting upon meeting of course informally: everything is cut and dried, even names and salaries of prospective officers are discussed and prejudged. Now, let there be an end to all this. Let us have no narrow issues. The betterment and advancement of the town provide a platform for the whole of the councillors to stand upon...'[17]

Most of the names of the first councillors could be traced back as prominent in the town at least to mid-century. They can be found as leaders in the violent and successful opposition to the proposal for a local Board of Health in 1849: the first attempt at improvement - if only for water supply, drainage and sewage disposal. These men were 'Natives', born and bred, who dominated the town, not only through the intricacies of family relationships but directly through business and employment. A tradesman who was not favoured soon went out of business. A professional man would quickly suffer from a want of clients. The story is told of a 'foreigner' who moved into Whitstable and opened a shop competing with existing tradesmen. Two old 'salts' leant on the wall either side of his premises and no one entered. After some weeks in despair he closed and left the town.

This aggressive attitude towards the newcomer, the 'foreigner', related historically to a deeply held distrust of the outsider which had arisen in a maritime community in which smuggling had long been regarded as a legitimate accompaniment of the seafaring life. Whilst the blatant ignoring of the law, as seen in the gangs typical of Thomas Reynold's day, had been suppressed, it is certainly a matter of local 'understanding' that on a smaller scale, quieter 'free trade' long continued, centred on the harbour.

Local government in Whitstable, therefore, reflected a high degree of parochialism and entrenched conservative attitudes which certainly prevailed until at least the Second World War. 'Procrastination', it was said, was the watchword of the Council: debate was never more heated than when they were discussing the cost of their cups of tea! Throughout these years the same local names recur in the records:

'During the first forty five years of the Whitsable Urban District Council itself there served as members of that body five Daniels, three Kemps, three Collars, two Goldfinches, two Ganns, two Fitts and two Reeves. A Daniels was the first Clerk. A Goldfinch was the first Surveyor. Kemps (father and son) had been the rate collectors. A Knowles was the first Inspector of Nuisances, and later became a councillor when he retired. Another Daniels had been clerk of the parish council, and also became a councillor after retirement from that office'.[18]

At these first meetings of the new local government for the town held in the Foresters Hall, the pattern for its future representative nature and effectiveness were set. Some townsmen did feel the need to keep an eye on the proceedings and so a larger meeting room was needed and a move was soon made to the Assembly Rooms.

1936: 'Blackshirts in Whitstable.

Of all the meetings which must have taken place over the years in the Foresters Hall - a place dedicated to 'the highest purposes of philanthropy' - none will seem more extraordinary to us today, than that of May 22nd 1936:[19]

'BLACKSHIRTS AND THE EMPIRE'

'Friendship with Germany Essential'

Thus headlined the Whitstable Times, beginning its lengthy report: 'A fighting speech was delivered by Mr William Joyce (Director of Propaganda, British Union of Fascists) at a largely attended meeting...' Joyce, of course, was to become notorious during the war for his broadcasts from Germany, his rasping voice gaining him the derisive nickname of 'Lord Haw-Haw'. In 1946 he was hanged as a traitor[20].

With the hindsight of later terrible and tragic events it is difficult now to believe that there were citizens of this little town who paraded in black shirts and called themselves Fascists. Equally difficult is it to understand why a large audience applauded the sentiments so eloquently expounded

A William Joyce (Lord Haw-Haw) Political meeting at the Horsebridge.

by Joyce: admiration for Hitler's Germany and his thinly disguised anti-semitism.

To get the local Fascists in context first - the only other reference to their activities ever made in the newspaper was the holding of a whist drive! To understand the applause from the audience one must look at the arguments of the address in the context of the mood of those pre-war years. These were times when many people felt demoralised and confused.

Joyce utilised a theme dear to the hearts of many speakers in the late 1930s: a harking back to the great days when Britain had been the dominant world power and the map of the world which hung in most schoolrooms was swathed in red from Canada across to India. 'I do not want to follow any foreign leader', declared Mr Joyce, 'I will not sit down in adulation of any foreigner, because I believe that what Britain does is done best of all...' and later, 'It is not for us to follow a foreign power, for ours will be a finer and greater than that...'

First, then, there was the theme of nationalism. And from this followed the parallel with Germany: the resurgence of a defeated nation under dynamic leadership, linked with its perceived role as the bulwark against Bolshevism - the bogy of the time. Second, against the background of world recession came the attack on exploitation by international finance 'under the control of Jewish financiers': the antisemitism crept into reasoned argument. Thirdly Joyce expounded his doctrine of 'Socialism': a rather vague idea of 'corporate trade' in which industries worked for the national good, collaborating through a Second Chamber which would replace the House of Lords. Behind the arguments was the force of rhetoric. Joyce concluded: 'Our people lack leadership but give them that and the inspiration of our great National Socialist creed and they will prove themselves once again the greatest people in the world.'

The appeal of this speech must be seen against the uncertainties which people in Whitstable, as elsewhere in the country, felt in 1936. Unemployment was high; the traditional industries had collapsed with little to take their place; there was widespread and acute poverty. A letter to the local paper dubbed Whitstable 'An antiquated, frowsy old town with no one to care for it', continuing that it was 25 years out of date - 'more like 250 years' came the retort next week. There was an 'Occupational Centre of Unemployed' in the town which kept idle hands busy with craft work and, just as in the old Victorian days, the New Year was celebrated with a charitable tea-party and entertainment for 200 families.

Uncertainty and alarm were generated by the conflicting views in political speeches made locally and reported in the press. The Navy League, advocating re-armament especially in the navy, greeted the New Year with the message: 'The word WAR has again been on all lips in the closing days of 1935'. In April Sir Stafford Cripps in Canterbury stated that 'It was no exaggeration to say that the state of nervous fear in Europe was greater than it had ever been'. The older generation of men in 1936 were those who had survived the slaughter of the War; and there was hardly a family in the land who had not lost husband, brother or friend in the fighting - 'Can that come about again?' they would ask. Advocating the economic co-operation of socialism (not Joyce's variety) and the pursuit of peace, he said, with more prescience than he realised: 'The tragedy today was that we are allowing ourselves to slip down the slope of carelessness and the slope of apathy which would inevitably end in the pit of destruction.' But the German annexation of the Rhineland and Italy's invasion of Abyssinia were unopposed; while at the League of Nations there was much talk of punitive sanctions and no agreement on action. In the face of force the world organization appeared impotent.

The message to a local youth rally of the Empire Day Movement was 'We must be prepared to preserve the liberties and peace of the world with arms in our hands'. The Navy League headlined the 'Futility of the League of Nations' and it was only the British navy that could 'guarantee our very existence'. In successive weeks the Tankerton Lecture Society listened to the theme of the 'Price of Peace' from the United Nations Union, and 'Armageddon' from one Brigadier-General Blakeney who expounded the view that 'there is nobody more traduced by the Press in this country and others than Herr Hitler. He is a man evidently with a mission... he had the whole of his people entirely with him, inspired with the magnificence of the ideals of service and discipline that he had put before them...'

If these views were listened to politely in places such as the Foresters Hall William Joyce and his cronies got short shrift when they tried soap-box oratory down at the Horsebridge. Apparently Joyce liked a drink at the Prince Albert and then...

'Outside he would harangue the crowd on the glories of his master's new Germany: a discourse which never quite convinced the Whitstable people.

'One day a henchman, in brand new black shirt, had taken up the rabble rousing, and was finding the 'rabble' anything but impressed.

'When he could not give a satisfactory answer to a question put by Captain Bully Finn, an ex-Commodore of the Anglo-American Oil Company, Bully felt it was time to demonstrate his disapproval.

'So he "upped" with his walking stick, and prodded the blackshirt in the stomach, toppled him off the box into the dust. Instantly chairs, pamphlets,

William Joyce - 'Lord Haw-Haw'[20]

Joyce was born of Irish parents who had emigrated to the United States. When he was three years old the family returned to Ireland. During the struggle for independence in 1920 his father, who was very pro-British, had his property burnt, and the boy William acted as an informer for the para-military 'Black and Tans' who ruthlessly hunted members of the independence movement. At this early age he was caught up in a struggle in which violence was used to settle political and personal scores.

With Irish independence the family left for England and out of his background the young William developed a passionate belief in 'King and Empire', with concepts of loyalty and service to a cause. First he enlisted in the army but was discharged as he was under age. Then he decided to follow an academic career, gaining a first-class degree in English at Birkbeck College, where he developed his debating skills as President of the Conservative Society.

With his very right-wing views Joyce was naturally attracted by Moseley's British Union of Fascists and as a brilliant writer and speaker he made rapid progress in the organisation, soon becoming Director of Propaganda. Hoping to make a visit to Germany Joyce applied for and was granted a British passport, incorrectly stating he was a British citizen. This was to prove his undoing when, after the war, he stood trial as a traitor. Joyce left England for Germany in August 1939 and in September he commenced his propaganda broadcasts: 'Germany calling...' he would begin. In 1945 as the end of the war was imminent, he was arrested trying to flee to neutral Sweden.

William Joyce was executed in January 1946.

and box went flying over T. Browning's fence.

'That was the end of Fascism in Whitstable. Haw-Haw was standing beside the dethroned balckshirt and got chased away in the melee.'[21]

What then was Joyce, by now something of a national figure, doing in Whitstable in 1936? For it seems he was certainly here for some months; he is remembered as working in a radio shop on Ludgate Hill (where the Starvation Point garden is today), and also in a bookshop in Canterbury. He frequented several pubs in the town; did he live locally? Inquiries as to Whitstable's connection with a man who is remembered as a traitor during the war have led to the response 'that's something best forgotten'. Perhaps at this time Joyce needed a break away from the limelight, for Fascist meetings were becoming increasingly violent; he also had some wealthy and influential supporters in East Kent, but with whom his connection was kept discreet.

In general, from the pages of the Whitstable Times for 1936 one gets the impression of a quiet community in which life seemed to revolve around the local sports teams and especially the three cinemas.

In July the rebuilt Oxford cinema was opened, seating 800 people in plush warm comfort; at the entrance a gold-braided commissionaire and within blue-uniformed usherettes received patrons to the 'picture palace' (now the Bingo Hall). At the same time in the High Street the Argosy was also being rebuilt (remaining today as the supermarket), and up at Tankerton was the giant Trocadero, a converted roller-skating rink which could seat 1000. Huge advertisements dominated the newspaper, the headlines enticing with stories of romance and adventure: an escapist world away from the often drab and worrying life outside.

There were some signs of change and talk of 'progress'. Under Slum Clearance Orders old cottages were being condemned and pulled down, but 'the destruction of the town as we Natives know it' was the cry. Road traffic was increasing: there were reports of fatal accidents on the new coastal road to Thanet, and local roads were being straightened and widened (happily the scheme to knock down one side of narrow Harbour Street did not prevail - just too expensive!). In the 20s and 30s the town area had begun to spread outwards with the laying out of housing estates, especially eastwards where the Tankerton Estate was now linked with developments in Swalecliffe and Chestfield, although in reality many of the new roads remained muddy tracks leading nowhere and houses stood isolated among many unsold building plots.

The population was therefore slowly increasing: the 1921 census recorded 9,842 for the area from Seasalter to Swalecliffe, and in 1931, 11,201. It was decreasing in the old town centre and increasing eastward at Tankerton. The need to co-ordinate services for these embryonic suburbs had led to a revision of local government boundaries and now the Urban District embraced the whole built-up area. With the increasing demand for administrative staff, the council had moved the previous year to new premises at 'The Castle', Tankerton.

As we saw, 1895 presented Whitstable with the challenge to launch effective representative local government: a process stultified by the continuation over decades of the interlocking influence of a few dominant families. Now 1936 offered the opportunity to create a cohesive urban area:

'The civic pride that we expected to find in the corporate unity represented by these combined areas is sadly wanting. Instead there is the regrettable spectacle of sectional interests clamouring for special consideration irrespective of the welfare of the town as a whole... In short there seems to be a general idea abroad that Whitstable is not a town but a series of separate communities, antagonistic, or at least indifferent, to the well-being of each other... Let us remember for good or ill the Urban District is now one and indivisible, a town, a civic entity, not a collection of villages.' (Arthur Collar)[22].

Anyone looking at the social institutions across the area today must agree that parochialism has prevailed: a process reinforced by the absorption of Whitstable into the Canterbury District Council in 1974. And where are we today? We are reconsidering the delegation of some authority locally: shall it be to a town council or to parish councils? We are back to the debate of 1894-5; as so often in human affairs, history turns full circle.

The Story of a Benefactor and the Birth of the Museum

On an evening in the early 1950s the crowds buzzed with anticipation as the Carnival procession approached. A visitor was puzzled by the leading vehicle, a large open car, in the back of which could be seen a tiny, wizened-looking figure with a long white beard. 'Who's that then? Looks like Methuselah!' Well not quite, but Fred Goldfinch, leading the way as Chairman of the organising committee was certainly not far off a century in age.

This veteran had become one of the grand old men of Whitstable: the kind of eccentric which our modern communities no longer produce. As 'Bicuits' Goldfinch he was known in the time honoured tradition that every 'Native' was given a nickname[23]. Fred was reputed to be one of the meanest of men: when making up sacks of ships biscuits at his grocer's shop he would carefully snap a biscuit in half to make the exact weight - no less, but certainly no more. Like all such local names it was used with the broad humour of a small community: there was no malice intended.

The Goldfinch name goes back in the town's history to at least 1800; the many branches of the family being involved in the various maritime activities which characterised Whitstable. Even today the sign 'Goldfinch Sails' stands out on one of the attractive old buildings along Sea Wall, although the last traditional sailmaker, Ray Goldfinch, retired back in 1965.

Fred Goldfinch was born in 1861 over his father's grocer's shop in Sydenham Street[24]. His earliest memory, he would recall, was of the great fire of November 1869, when flames swept through the area on the western side of the harbour, destroying about a third of Sea Wall and Harbour Street. It was the most destructive of Whitstable's numerous conflagrations. As Fred recalled:

'He was awakened by his brother, who shouted that the house was alight. Fortunately his brother's warning was an exaggeration, but an excusable one. The wind was blowing inshore and a great shower of burning confetti, as it seemed, was flaking down across the town, falling on the Goldfinch house and the surrounding district.

'The burning area included dozens of stores, sheds, wooden houses - most of them tarred - and many shanty constructions for boats and tackle. They were well alight, crackling and falling.'

There was no loss of life, and prompt action by many townsfolk in removing the stock of gunpowder from the divers' store - it was used for blasting wrecks which were a hazard to shipping - saved the town from a shattering explosion which could have had devastating consequences.

Over the remaining years of the nineteenth century and half way through the twentieth - for 'Biscuits' died aged 95 in 1956 - Fred Goldfinch became involved in virtually every aspect of the town's business and community life. Following his father he became a ship and barge owner; he was regarded as an authority on sailing ships and had a fine collection of paintings of the many vessels which plied from Whitstable waters. He was a keen yachtsman and a founder member of the Yacht Club. He bought and sold property, as in everything else with a keen eye for a good bargain. He and his builder partner George Porter built Wave Crest, the only real attempt to promote seaside boarding house property in Whitstable. Amongst his many speculations was to buy an apparently useless narrow triangle of land lying between the ends of Sea Street and Harbour Street, known locally as 'Starvation Point'. But in response to the challenge 'Even you can't make anything out of that, Fred,' it is said he set to there and then and sketched out a design on the back of an envelope and had it built. The tall curiously castellated Harbour Buildings date from 1905, and whether successful or not immediately, in 1912 it was developed by couturier Wallace Pring to become the most high-class shop in town. Another triangle of land up at Tankerton Circus he gave to the town to be laid out as a garden, though some said only because even 'Biscuits' could not fit a house on that site!

For some year Fred Goldfinch was a Director of the Oyster Fishery Company, the successor to the great 'Company of Free Fishers and Dredgers' which made the Whitstable native oyster world-famous. In 1894 when local government came to the town Fred was one of the first twelve councillors to be elected and he it was who designed the crest for the new council: appropriately for a maritime town a ship's wheel with twelve spokes representing the councillors, and in the centre a brigantine in full sail. For many years he was Chairman of the Entertainments Committee and was instrumental in establishing the skating rink at Reeves Beach which was a very popular rendezvous just before and during the First World War. And finally one may recall that he was one of the prime movers to give the town its own hospital. During the War a number of houses and what is now the Marine Hotel were used to treat wounded soldiers, and local people felt that this medical facility should be retained when war ended. So in April 1918 one half of the 'Marine' was kept as a Cottage Hospital, and then a scheme was launched to raise £10,000 to fund a new building. The whole town was galvanised into every possible means of fund raising. The Committee's secretary was Fred Goldfinch, and on December 8th 1926 Whitstable's Cottage Hospital was opened.

Like many townsfolk Fred Goldfinch had a great pride in the achievements and history of his town, though, as we have seen in Chapter Four, the belief in tracing the history of Whitstable back to Domesday was based on a mis-reading of the evidence. As in many towns in the Victorian period there was a move in 1885 to establish a small museum. The Assembly Rooms down at the Horsebridge were being extended for the Institute, a men's club which provided one room for smoking, chess and the newspapers, and now the second reading room would contain a library and the collection: 'the walls being well furnished with cases containing fossil remains... insects, British birds, antiques of various kinds and one devoted to objects of a more miscellaneous character'[25]. This was very typical of the time with the Victorian emphasis on the gaining of knowledge and self-improvement. The little museum did not apparently meet with immediate enthusiasm and some months later a rather caustic criticism appeared in the local press: 'Perhaps Whitstable people prefer bones with something on them, and jugs with something in them, to the rare and ancient specimens which they are invited to admire.'

Quite what happened over the intervening years is not clear, but in 1947 a small group of business men, keen to promote the history of Whitstable came together to promote the establishment of a new museum; one of these being Fred Goldfinch. Land was purchased, a design proposed and the collection of exhibits grew, but sadly the scheme was not realised. Meanwhile the collection was housed in a series of rather unsuitable locations where damage and loss occurred. However Fred Goldfinch had set up Trusts in his name and that of his wife with the object of creating this long-sought-after objective, and so in 1985, nearly 30 years after his death, the town's museum was opened through the dedication of a group of Trustees in collaboration with the City Council. The building was still owned by the Foresters, though since 1914 it had been leased to the British Legion[26]. Much of the finance, £40,000, came from the Goldfinch Trusts and a further grant of £30,000 enabled the splendid little art gallery to be added later. So at long last through the thriftiness of 'Biscuits' Goldfinch the town gained a most important and attractive amenity.

The life of 'Biscuits' Goldfinch has not been told because it was unique, but rather because he typified many of those who were part of the Whitstable community in the days when it was still a very small town: a place in which people lived and worked; where there were inextricable links between the place and the people - when half the town seemed to be related to the other half.

Fred Goldfinch was a Whitstable 'Native' born and bred, and lived in the town all his life. In the 1860s and 70s, as a boy, he experienced the days when the maritime character of the town was at its peak. He must have heard many a tale from the old 'salts' of dangers and disasters at sea and memories of the 'free trade' of smuggling in its heyday. By the end of the last century he had become one of the leading men in Whitstable, elected to serve as one of the first councillors. Yet having spent little less than half-a-century in the Victorian years, Fred Goldfinch lived on for just over half of the twentieth century and so experienced the events described here and which are illustrated in many of the exhibits in the museum. He saw the little town become a sprawling urban area and even Fred Goldfinch, in his final years, abandoned the old town centre for the 'suburb' of Tankerton.

Here then at the museum this exploration of local history is concluded. For the enthusiast there are the many exhibits to study; there are numerous books and articles to read, there are still boxes of records to catalogue and examine, and there are the byways and buildings which can be related to the past. Local history offers an endless exploration of 'places' and 'people'.

References

1. Deeds of the Whitstable Museum, Canterbury City Council.
2. **Reynold's smuggling gang**, personal information Mr Wallace Harvey.
3. Douch J, '**Rough Rude Men - A History of Old-time Kentish Smuggling**', Crabwell/Buckland Publications Dover 1985.
   Harvey W, 'The **Seasalter Company - A Smuggling Fraternity** 1740-1854' Emprint Whitstable 1983.
4. Quoted in Harvey ref. 3 above.
5. Goodsall RH, '**Whitstable, Seasalter and Swalecliffe - The History** of Three Kent Parishes', Cross and Jackman Canterbury 1938, Chap XVI 'Smuggling'.
6. WT 8.1.1876, obituary of **Robert Tritton Whorlow**.
7. WT 18.9.1915, obituary of **Albert Whorlow**.
8. Pike G, Page M, Cann J, 'Ales and Tales - Pubs in the Story of Whitstable', Whitstable Improvement Trust 1993, Chap. 6 '**From Street to Town**'.
9. **Trustees of the Whitstable Charities**, Minute Book 1844-50, Whitstable Museum

Wallace Harvey collection.
10. Gosden PH, '**Friendly Societies in England 1815-1875**', Manchester University Press 1960.
11. Whitstable Times reports on the **Foresters**: decision to purchase the hall 12.3.1880; description of the refurbished hall 7.5.1880; Grand Opening with Brother Coleman's speech 25.5.1880.
12. WT reports of **distress in Whitstable** - quotation 13.3.1880; 24.1.1880.
13. WT: town meeting 26.4.1879. The following details of organisations using the new hall are taken from this newspaper.
14. For the character of **licensed premises** in the town, see ref. 8. above.
15. WT: **Urban District Council** - boundaries considered 21.7.1894 and correspondence in subsequent weeks; candidates 8.12.1894; first meeting 5.1.1895
16. Gray RA, '**The Social and Economic History of Whitstable** with particular reference to local government and administration', MA thesis UKC 1970, especially chapters 6, 7 and 13.
17. WT 5.1.1895, letter signed 'Progressive'.
18. Gray RA, ref. 16 above p.334.
19. WT 30.5.1936.
20. Cole JA, '**Lord Haw-Haw and William Joyce**', Faber 1964.
21. Woodman G & G, '**We Remember Whitstable**', Pryor Publications Whitstable 2nd ed. 1988, pp.68-69.
22. WT 7.3.1936, letter signed Arthur Collar.
23. Woodman G & G ref. 21 above, for many examples of nicknames pp.93-101.
24. WT 17.11.1956, **obituary of Fred Goldfinch**. Description of the fire in Woodman G & G, ref. 23 above, p.15. For a detailed account of the fire of 1869 see ref. 8 above, Chapter 7, 'The Town Alight'.
25. WT 25.4.1885 and letter commenting 5.9.1885.
26. WT 25.4.1985 (**general history of the Museum site**), and 2.5.85 (opening ceremony).

A CHRONOLOGIGAL INDEX

GENERAL INDEX

ILLUSTRATIONS, MAPS AND DIAGRAMS